instant JAPAN

by

Masahiro Watanabe

and

Bruce Rogers

HEIAN INTERNATIONAL, INC.

INSTANT JAPAN

By Masahiro Watanabe and Bruce Rogers

ISBN No.0-89346-181-4
Library of Congress Catalog No. 77-115002

Revised and First American Edition: 1981

HEIAN INTERNATIONAL INC.
P.O. Box 2402
South San Francisco, CA 94080

Printed in United States.

CONTENTS

CONTENTS

AUTHOR'S NOTE

Just prior to the 1964 Tokyo Olympic Games, I wrote the little book, *INSTANT JAPANESE* in collaboration with my good friend, Kei Nagashima. I have been most gratified that this minor opus has been one of the best-selling books to visitors to Japan. I wonder why this was so. There are many other better books written by linguistics scholars; why was this one so popular? One reason must be that neither Kei nor I were language professors, and our purchasers weren't linguists either. Visitors to Japan aren't interested in really learning the language, but do want to know a few words and phrases to open the doors of friendship. Another reason may be that both of us were Japanese and we truly wanted the visitor to love our small island country. On every page, between the lines, we tried to put in our own feelings.

We felt it would benefit our readers further

to introduce Japan in our next book, *INSTANT JAPAN.* As we were planning and discussing this new book, Kei suddenly passed away. I lost my best friend and co-author, and at first, I thought of giving up the idea of doing it. But such a large number of interested visitors will be coming to our shores, I feel that it is almost a duty to put out iNSTANT JAPAN, and am sure that Kei would surely agree.

I chose Bruce Rogers to be my new co-author; he has been my friend since 1937, he likes Japan and loves the people, and has lived here since 1938. He is a "foreigner" (he dislikes the word) who knows our country very well, and most of the book is his doing. We have had much discussion (as did Kei Nagashima and I), and there are, of course, a number of differences of opinion between us. But it seems to me to be best to leave most of his opinions as he expressed them since I am sure that our readers would like to hear the opinions of one of the foreigners who like and live in Japan.

Please read both INSTANT JAPANESE and INSTANT JAPAN, and get the feeling of "Our Japan" and "Their Japan." This may bring you closer to the "Real Japan," and we both sincerely hope that you will like the country and people of Japan as we both do.

Masahiro Watanabe

PREFACE

This little book is not for the scholar—or even for the square! There are plenty of far more erudite tomes on all phases of Japanese life, history, and culture, and the visitor to Japan who wants to find out how other visitors to Japan have attempted to explain the inexplicable is referred to other books. Our more modest aim is simply to give the tourist a quick impression of the country—a "once over lightly," so to speak—and to tell him things we think will make his stay more pleasant. Japan is one of the most difficult countries in the world to know—a fact long-term residents delight in pointing out—and one of the most agreeable to visit, as you are about to discover for yourself.

So put this book in your pocket and make use of it while you travel about. But for heaven's sake don't throw it away as you board your plane at Haneda. Take it home. Amaze your friends and neighbors with the wealth of

information about Japan that you've acquired. (Incidentally, you might also find it useful as you run through those color slides that wild horses probably won't keep you from showing at the drop of a light switch.)

The companion volume, *Instant Japanese*, is no more pretentious than this one. It doesn't guarantee to teach you to speak flawless Japanese, but it will help you to make friends as you travel about and so give you a more rewarding trip. With this book in one pocket and *Instant Japanese* in another, you should never find yourself at a loss—but if you do, some cheerful, smiling Japanese who speaks a bit of English will very soon be solving all your problems for you. Including where to find the driest martini in town.

AUTHOR'S FOREWORD

Since you are reading these words, it seems a fairly safe assumption that you are either in Japan already or are on your way. In the latter case, perhaps a few words about what to expect on arrival might be in order. If you are here already, you know the worst—and the best. You know that you must be armed with a variety of documents and that you must satisfy customs regulations—and you also know that the Japanese will do their best to make things easy for you.

Let's take the documents first. Naturally you know you have to have a valid passport, but unless your country has a treaty with Japan that eliminates visas, your passport—no matter how valid it is—won't get you into Japan unless it has already been stamped by a Japanese consulate outside the country. (Britons don't need visas; Americans do.)

Another document you will have to have is a

validated certificate that you have been vaccinated against smallpox within the past three years, and if you have been passing through a region declared cholera-infected, you will have to bring proof that you have been inoculated against cholera as well. The customary form of these validations is a yellow booklet called "International Certificates of Vaccination." If, you are continuing onward from Japan to a cholera-infected area, you will need the same certificate.

Customs ought to offer no problem. There may be a cursory inspection, but usually there is none, and you'll be allowed to bring in duty-free, as your airline hostess will already have explained, a carton of cigarettes and three bottles of liquor. Importation of gold, narcotics, and weapons is prohibited—and smuggling, in Japan as elsewhere, is punishable.

But let's assume you have no Smith and Wesson in your shoulder holster, no gold bars strapped across your chest, not even any grass in your pocket. You have passed customs in-

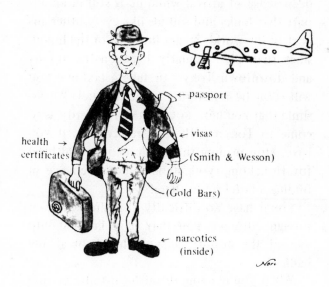

← passport

← visas

health →
certificates

(Smith & Wesson)

(Gold Bars)

← narcotics
(inside)

Nori

13

spection triumphantly, all your documents are in order, and Japan has opened her doors for you. You have arrived! Actually, of course, you are still at the airport—and no one feels any deep sense of arrival while he is still in an airport that looks and sounds like every other airport in the world. So get into one of the limousines that ply regularly between the airport and downtown Tokyo or take a taxi and you will soon be registering at your hotel. We assume that you have not been so foolhardy as to come to Tokyo without a reservation; if you have, stop reading this book at once and head for Hongkong—you stand a better chance of finding a hotel room there!

You'll have no difficulty changing whatever foreign currency you may have brought into yen—at the airport, at your hotel, or at any bank.

When you're going through Customs, be sure to pick up what is called a "tax-free form." This entitles you, as a non-resident, to buy cameras, transistor radios, pearls, and the like without paying a luxury tax. All your purchases of such items are entered on this form, which you must show to Customs on your departure. Otherwise, you will have to pay the tax you didn't pay when you did your carefree buying.

As to whether you should keep receipts for all the things you bought, to show the Customs inspectors in your own country, there seem to be two schools of thought. One subscribes to the theory that you have a fifty-fifty chance the inspector will value your purchases lower than the price you actually paid; the other, more pessimistic school says that if you produce the receipts, the inspector won't make a higher valuation.

But that momentous decision, we trust, is still a long way off—you have just arrived in Japan, an exciting and fascinating country is waiting for you. unique experiences lie ahead, and

Welcome to Japan!!

Bruce Rogers

1. GEOGRAPHY
AND
CLIMATE

GEOGRAPHY AND CLIMATE

Like Hawaii, Japan is a group of islands—or, as more learned folk would have it—an archipelago, no doubt thrust up above the surface of the sea in the dim past through volcanic action. Japan's main islands are only four in number, and they are surrounded by some two thousand smaller islands that dot the surface of the sea nearby.

If your stay is to be a short one, chances are you will visit only Honshu, the largest of the four islands and the one that has the greatest concentration of population. The crowded cities of Tokyo, Kyoto, Nagoya, Osaka, and Hiroshima are all on the island of Honshu.

Hokkaido is the northernmost of the main islands and is also the most sparsely settled; it is largely given over to fishing, forestry, and agriculture—though Japanese industry, thrusting as it does now in all directions, has begun to invade Hokkaido too. Hokkaido is probably best known for the fact that it is the home of the few Caucasian aborigines left in Japan, the Ainu; unlike the rest of the country, they are a hairy people, and they have preferred to maintain their primitive way of life. Most Ainu have, as a matter of fact, married other Japanese and been absorbed into the mainstream of Japanese life—but there are a few carefully preserved "native" villages, whose inhabitants make their living out of a thriving tourist trade, Japanese and foreign. Hokkaido has a short summer and a long winter, with lots of snow; spring and autumn can be extremely beautiful. Its climate is, in fact, very much like that of the south coastal region of Alaska.

Proceeding southward, we cross the straits to the main island of Honshu, which is far warmer than Hokkaido and grows progressively warmer the farther south we go. Tokyo's climate is not unlike that of New York or Washington, though its winters are considerably warmer than New York's and most of its summers cooler than Washington's. Tokyo seldom sees enough snow during the winter months for it to remain on the ground, though occasionally the city is blanketed in white and occasionally too, ponds and puddles are thinly coated with ice. During the summer, the temperature almost never rises above ninety degrees Fahrenheit, but in July and August the "discomfort index," as some people call it, is not unlike Washington's. In other words, as a few gasping, sweat-drenched tourists have been heard to remark, "It's not the heat so much as the humidity." Spring and autumn in Tokyo are mild and remarkably pleasant.

The southern island of Kyushu and the eastern island of Shikoku have been called sub-tropical, but this is something of an exaggeration—though they are certainly warmer than their northern neighbors and see a good deal more rain. The fact that they lie in the typhoon path also tends to increase the annual precipitation.

South of Kyushu, the archipelago continues on to the Ryukyus, including Okinawa, that controversial area which temporarily passed from Japanese to American control after the end of the Pacific War and which has since been returned to Japan.

The total area of Japan is about 143,000 square miles (roughly the same as that of Montana), and its total population is just over a hundred million—of which more than ten per cent cluster in and around Tokyo, living and working there. With one of the densest concentrations of population in the world, Tokyo has nowhere to go but up—and that's what it has begun to do. Five other cities—Yokohama, Nagoya, Osaka, Kyoto, and Kita Kyushu—all have populations that are well over a million.

When one considers that a hundred million people live in an area of less than 150,000 square miles, one must also bear in mind that only a very small percentage (about 20%) of that area is usable for agriculture, industry, or habitation, since Japan is extremely mountainous. Thus the visitor is faced almost immediately by a problem that the Japanese have solved fairly satisfactorily long ago: how to live and work in extremely crowded conditions. There is seldom a vacant seat in a Japanese train; the visitor, therefore, is well advised to reserve a place ahead of time whenever he can. And when he makes his first visit to a department store, he may decide that the store owners have decided to sell everything at half-price that day, or even give it all away—but he will soon discover that the stores are crowded every day and all day. As for living conditions in the large cities, the average room in the average Japanese house is far smaller than anything the Westerner might have imagined possible. It will not take him long to realize how admirably the Japanese have solved this problem of over-crowding, and—unless he foolishly decides to tackle a subway during the rush hour—he will be neither jostled nor trampled nor suffocated by the hundred million busy, energetic people around him.

As for what clothes the visitor ought to bring with him, that must depend, naturally, to a large extent on what parts of the country he intends to visit and the time of year he plans to come. If Hokkaido in mid-winter sounds attractive, then of course he will want his heaviest overcoat; if his intention is to spend the summer months in Tokyo and Osaka or Kyoto, he will want light-weight shirts, and his wife will want to bring her thinnest dresses—all preferably drip-dry. Otherwise, the combined laundry and luggage problem might become a disagreeable one. The Japanese tend to dress more formally than Westerners. Men wear dark suits and seldom appear in public in the cities without a tie. One convention that has been accepted is that during the hot summer months, men may wear short-sleeved shirts (white, of course), but here again a tie is expected, and some of the more elegant bars and restaurants—no matter how hot it may be outside—won't serve men without coats. Being Japanese, of course, the management has a collection of jackets to lend thoughtless foreigners. During the hot pair of months, all bars and restaurants are air-conditioned, as are most taxis—so the problem is chiefly one of getting from your air-conditioned hotel room to an

air-conditioned taxi to an air-conditioned restaurant. Doesn't sound like much of a problem, does it? It isn't, either—except at certain
times of day when taxis are hard to come by.

One further word about Japan's hundred
million. The question here—as it is in most other
countries of the world—is how are you going to
keep them down on the farm? The phenomenal
growth of Japanese industry after the end of
the war has tended more and more to attract
youth away from the traditional occupations
of the Japanese people—rice farming, fishing,
and the like—to the large industrial complexes.
where pay is better, opportunity is virtually unlimited, and there are five or six movie houses
just around the corner—not to mention bars,
pachinko parlors, and other diversions. It has
been estimated that perhaps by the beginning
the next century Japan will be one large city—
and the estimate does not seem outrageous.
She will be, as indeed she has been for a number of years, dependent on imported raw
materials; in return, she may have surpassed

the United States in industrial production.

2. *HISTORY AND CULTURE*

HISTORY AND CULTURE

Who are they, then, these extraordinary people, unique among Asians in their vitality and energy and determination? How have they accomplished the various "miracles" that comprise their strange and sometimes incredible history? What mixture of races produced them?

The answer, of course, as always, is that there is no answer. The nearest we can get to one, so far, is to say that sometime around the beginning of the New Stone Age, tribes from both North-East and South-East Asia merged—for protection perhaps, perhaps for survival—and they also found the inviting, soft-green islands of the southern archipelago. Which came first, the merger or the migration, it is impossible to say. Perhaps they met on the mainland and crossed the Korean Strait together, perhaps they came in separate groups and founded their small tribal communities, only gradually discovering that hostility was not essential to their way of life. Whatever the process, the merger, as everyone agrees, turned out in the end to be a successful one.

It is most improbable that the Japanese islands were inhabited during the Old Stone Age: no pottery or any other trace of a paleolithic people has yet been found; but two types of New Stone Age pottery are fairly common. Then, around the time that the folk of the Middle East were hearing strange tales of a man who said he was God, in the Far East the new metal, bronze, was being brought from the mainland over to Japan, where the people were still living in small communities made up of a few family groups (called *uji*). But the Bronze Age was not destined to a very long life in Japan; iron soon took its place; and about the time that the Emperor Constantine declared Christianity to be the official religion of the Roman Empire, the small Japanese communities had acquired sufficient cohesion to form their first stable government. This was the Yamato court, in what is now Nara Prefecture, founded around the beginning of the fourth century by the man whom the Chinese called the Great Wa and the Japanese, Hatsu-kunishirasu-sumera-mikoto. (The reader will note that the Japanese, even in those early days, tended to be rather a long-winded people.)

In any case, the founder of Yamato was soon transmogrified into the Emperor Jimmu or (according to some historians) the Emperor Sujin, the grandson of the grandson of the Goddess of the Sun and the founder of the Imperial House. Jimmu is, of course, as mythical as his divine ancestress, though for many long years it was as dangerous to doubt his existence in Japan as in Europe it was to suggest that the earth revolved around the sun. In any case, the first Yamato ruler was in a very real sense the founder of his country. The Japanese still call themselves the Yamato race.

Perhaps a word is in order here about the Japanese system of chronology, which the visitor may at first find somewhat confusing. When an heir to the Japanese throne is born, he is, of course, given a name by which he is known to the people, but the moment he ascends the throne the name ceases to be used in public. During the years of his reign, he is known simply as Tennô (the Emperor) or Tennô Heika (His Majesty the Emperor); at the same time, the moment he ascends the throne, he announces what his *posthumous* name will be. After his death, it is the name by which he will be known to history; but during his lifetime, it is the name by which his reign is known—and dates in Japan are generally calculated as occurring in a certain year of a certain reign. Thus, the present Emperor (the 124th, according to legend) chose Showa ("Enlightened Peace") as his posthumous name, and therefore the present year of 1977 is known in Japan as Showa 52. No Japanese speaks of the reigning monarch as Hirohito; before the occupation, in fact, many Japanese had probably never even used the name. If, now, they no longer think of the Emperor as a divine personage, they see him as warmhearted, kindly, well-disposed. The divinity that hedged him in the past is gone; affection has taken its place.

HISTORY AND CULTURE

The older generation has not forgotten that at the most crucial moment in the life of the country, it was the unique relationship between the Emperor and the people that enabled Japan to surrender to the Allied powers without being annihilated by civil war. The older generation has not forgotten that if Japan not only continues to exist but also to thrive as she has never thriven, then Tennô Heika is due a considerable share of gratitude. The younger generation has other things on its mind—such as whether to get mixed up in tomorrow's *demo* (a Japanese word now meaning "demonstration") or whether to stay home and study for those all-important examinations. One thing that hasn't changed—despite war, defeat, and occupation—is the prestige of education. One recent lady-tourist who got into conversation with the waitress at her regular coffee-bar was surprised to learn that the girl was taking advanced courses in microbiology. She was even more surprised when the girl invited her to join the Chinese cooking class she went to twice a week!

We seem to have strayed quite a way from the capsule history of Japan that we started out on—but perhaps the distance is not all that great, for the continuity of Japanese history is more remarkable than the revolutionary changes that from time to time have shaken the country and left it gasping. Then once the cataclysm was over, Japan discovered that she was much the same Japan she had always been—save that she had somehow absorbed a foreign idea or technique during the process and made it her own. The introduction of Buddhism in the seventh century is as good an example as the introduction of automation in the twentieth.

It was during the two or three centuries that followed the foundation of the Yamato court that Buddhism crossed the water from Korea and China. Before its introduction, Japan's ancient religion had been Shinto -- though old Shinto was not quite what the foreigner thinks of today as a religion, largely because it laid down no commandments or restrictions. It was, rather, a means for the people to express their devotion to the varied manifestations of nature: these, called *kami*, might range all the way from the powerful Goddess of the Sun, to whom Japan was especially dear, to a great tree or a waterfall, a revered ancestor, or a monkey scurrying through the trees, carrying a message of great importance.

No doubt, after the establishment of the Yamato court, Japan was ready for the greater sophistication of Buddhism and Confucianism, the one born in India, the other in China, and both imported to Japan by way of Korea, the country's chief contact with the rest of the world.

Confucianism may be thought of as a system of morality rather than a revealed religion, a set of Spartan precepts for every-day living. It filled a need that the growing country was beginning to experience, and for a time Confucian morality was accepted in Japan as the only suitable way of life. Although children still study the *Analects*, contemporary Japan is no more bound by the precepts of the ancient Chinese sage than the West by the even harsher dictates of St. Paul.

Buddhism filled a different need and became a far more potent influence; in fact, it is still probably the most vital single spiritual force in Japanese life. Although it is splintered now into numerous sects (including Zen), there is an underlying unity based on the life of the founder. The visitor to Japan today, going from temple to temple, admiring the treasures the monks have accumulated, and watching the often highly complicated ritual that is enacted in the sanctuaries and attended by laity as well as clergy, will have no doubt that he is observing a still vital force in action. It is interesting to note that many Japanese households have two shrines -- one devoted to Shinto, where births, marriages, deaths, and other events of similar importance are reported to the ancestors; and one Buddhist altar, where the family hopes to insure a better life for its members in future incarnations.

Most birth and wedding ceremonies are performed within the Shinto ritual, and funerals are almost always a Buddhist ceremonial. The Japanese do not consider this a conflict of loyalty or faith. Performance of Buddhist ritual is less a worship of the Buddhist pantheon than a means of showing respect to one's ancestors. Shinto ceremonies are almost exactly the same in spirit. The deities of Shintoism are gods, not a God, and the gods are the revered ancestors of the Japanese. Yasukuni Shrine dedicated to the unknown soldier; Nogi Shrine in memory of General Nogi; and Togo Shrine in honor of Admiral Togo are examples of this ancestor respect. The Japanese do not consider these individuals as "Creators" but respect them as great personages of the race.

Although, to the ancient Japanese, the Buddhist images that came from Korea were alien and unfamiliar figures, expressing an alien philosophy and culture, the Japanese welcome was a warm one, first in the Imperial court, then later by the whole people. Soon there were Buddhist temples to be seen all over Yamato.

Equally important was the fact that with the acceptance of Buddhism came an ever-increasing interest in the complex court ceremony and ritual of the mainland. As a result, the old system of changing the capital with the accession of a new emperor had to be changed: it simply became too unwieldy, with the elaborate costumes and court furniture that were now considered essential. The Empress-Regnant Gemmyo, accordingly, established the first "permanent" capital, which she called Heijo-kyo and which we call Nara.

Seven successive emperors had their palaces there, and under their influence Buddhism prospered: temples were built, images were carved and painted, poems were written and collected. One major collection of poetry, the Manyōshū, has survived, as has the great bronze Buddha, or Daibutsu, of Nara. The years encompassed by these seven reigns are known in Japanese art history as the Nara Period.

Why Emperor Kammu decided to leave Nara and build a new capital elsewhere is uncertain. Some historians say that the chief Buddhist monks of Nara had grown so rich and powerful that they offered a threat to Imperial rule.

Whatever his reasons, Kammu at first considered Nagaoka-kyo and then, a few years later, fixed on a site watered by two rivers and surrounded by mountains. He called it Heiankyo, and we, for that reason, call the period of art that the new capital inaugurated the Heian, although we call the city itself Kyoto. The emperors lived there, more or less permanently, from 794, when the city was founded, until 1868, when Emperor Meiji moved his capital to Tokyo. It must be borne in mind, however, that the Heian Period is thought of as ending at the close of the twelfth century, when the shogunate military regime was established in Kamakura.

They were years of remarkable productivity

in all phases of Japanese life, years that fashioned the matrix in which the Japanese soul is still formed – despite all the cataclysmic changes that have occured since the close of the Heian Period. Many of the emperors and empresses were highly intelligent people, interested in the arts as well as in the new religion and the serious business of good government, in which they tended – or, at any rate, tried – to follow the precepts of Confucius.

It was during these years also that the distinctions between Buddhism and Shinto became less and less clear in the minds of the people. Buddhism, continuing to increase in popularity, evolved the theory that the *kami* of Shinto were in reality only further manifestations of the Buddha himself. The two religons very nearly became one. Later, the government issued an edict, defining and separating them, but the edict has been less effective than the near amalgamation. That is why, if you ask the Japanese tourist standing next to you, whether you are in a Shinto shrine or a Buddhist temple, sometimes he may, with some embarassment, have to admit that he doesn't know.

The Heian Period saw the establishment of the first national university as well as of provincial colleges – the initial symptoms, perhaps, of the Japanese passion for education. Everybody, from the emperor down, began to write poetry, and poetry-reading parties were everyday occurrences. At least two works of literature of abiding interest were produced during those years: Lady Murasaki's "Tale of Genji" and Sei-Shonagon's "Pillow Book (Makura no Soshi)." Sculptors and artists were kept busy decorating not only the temples and shrines of the capital but also the palaces of the nobles, whose life grew ever more sumptuous as the period drew to a close.

Perhaps it was this very fact – that the nobles were more interested in concerts and poetry-reading and flower-viewing (and love-making too) than in governing the country – that resulted finally in the establishment of a military dictatorship in Kamakura. The emperors, with their courts, were to continue for the next seven centuries to lead their indolent, beautiful lives in Kyoto, and although the emperors, direct descendants of the Goddess of the Sun, were still theoretically supreme, the actual power was now in the hands of the shogun (or generalissimo) who established his military headquarters at Kamakura and from there effectively ruled the country, collecting taxes and overseeing, with increasing severity, the daily life of the people.

It was during the military rule of the shogunate (which lasted for nearly seven centuries) that Japan's feudal society become so firmly established that vestiges of it still color the life and thinking of the people. Although rigid class distinction has been largely abolished, every Japanese is nevertheless always conscious of the precise nature of his relationship toward every other Japanese with whom he comes in contact. He knows what his duties and obligations are and he knows he is expected to abide by them; he also expects the same of everyone else. Merchants, who were at the bottom of the social ladder during feudalism, are now, in the new industrial society, at the top – but each, whether he be a company president or a section chief, knows exactly how low and how often he should bow in greeting a colleague.

These observations refer, of course, only to Japanese; the foreigner need not concern himself with them because, no matter how long he may live in the country, he never becomes a Japanese. He is always an outsider and so is not bound by the rules that bind the Japanese. This too is a result of the centuries of feudalism, when the country was virtually cut off from the rest of the world. Japan, during those seven centuries, was wholly self-contained and was content to be so – more than content, she insisted on it. Except for very brief periods she adamantly rejected all intercourse with all other countries. It could only result, the shogunate decided, in contamination.

Japanese were forbidden to leave Japan, and

within the country itself their movements were restricted by a system of passports and checkpoints. It was a cramped life, to be sure, and often, particularly for those who were not samurai, a cruel one – yet it was also, on the whole, a quiet time, enabling the arts of peace to flourish, not only painting and sculpture and literature but also such crafts as weaving and dyeing, metalwork and pottery. It was the existence of a large, highly skilled group of artisans that enabled Japan, once she determined in 1868 to become a modern nation, to accomplish in a few years what had taken centuries in the West.

Japan's feudal era is customarily divided into several periods, and modern-day scholars wrangle ceaselessly about precisely what those periods were and when they began and when they ended. It is not a controversy we shall make any attempt to resolve; in fact, we shall do our best to avoid it.

Let us simply take note that the first period, the Kamakura, began sometime around the close of the twelfth century when Yoritomo, the scion of the Minamoto clan, was appointed by the Emperor to be Sei-i-Tai-shôgun ("barbarian-subduing generalissimo") and established his military camp at Kamakura. It was a crucial moment in the life of Japan, for the seat of power now shifted from the Imperial Palace in Kyoto to the *bakufu* (or "camp office") at Kamakura. The emperors were never to know true power again (for even after the so-called Meiji restoration in 1868, constitutional goverment gradually replaced autocratic rule), but throughout those centuries they remained the symbols of Japan. Though stripped of power, they still, in a Japanese way, retained the supreme power: they were the possessors of the unique entity it has now become fashionable to call "charisma." Even today's young people, who affect to be disinterested in the Emperor, would feel uneasy if the compound within the Imperial moat no longer housed the familiar symbol. It is interesting to note, in this connection, that Japan's small but highly vociferous minority of radical students who are opposed to continuance of the Security Treaty with the United States violently attack government installations of all sorts but keep their eyes turned away, just as their grandfathers did, from the Imperial Palace.

The Kamakura Period, which lasted for about a century and a half, saw the beginning of stern military control by the shogun over the whole country, it saw the emergence of the spartan spirit of *bushido* (the way of the warrior) which was to play so important a role in the coming centuries, and it saw also the development of a new kind of art – an art that was not, like the more effete art of Kyoto, derived from China but that tried to express the new virile spirit of the new Japan.

The fall of Kamakura as the seat of power began with the attempted invasion of the country by the Yuan dynasty of China, descendants of Genghis Khan. The first invasion sent by his grandson, Kublai Khan, was repulsed; then, in 1281, came a second army a hundred thousand strong. Once again the Japanese were victorious, aided in large part by a violent typhoon, which they called a *kamikaze* (divine wind). Despite the victory, however, the Kamakura government was too impoverished to reward its army adequately; discontent mounted; and the emperor, together with his nobles and a few generals, plotted the overthrow of the Kamakura government.

When the shogun learned of the plot, he exiled the emperor to a small island in the Japan Sea, but the latter escaped and eventually led a victorious army against the shogun. The emperor's restoration to power was a brief one, however, and he was forced again to flee Kyoto. He established his court at Yoshino, while a new emperor was invested at Kyoto, with the result that for fifty-seven years the country had two imperial courts, the one at Kyoto being called the Northern court, the other the Southern. But neither court wielded real power in the country: that was held by the Ashikaga general named Takauji, who set up his own military government in Kyoto. It remained within the Ashikaga clan until the end of the sixteenth century, a period known as the Muromachi (after the district of Kyoto in which the Ashikaga *bakufu* was established).

Without going into the complex and – save to a student of Japanese history, perhaps – the very boring family rivalries that characterized the period, we may note that despite the ceaseless hostility, it was a period of unparalleled artistic activity. Most of the many facets of Japan's present-day cultural life were either carved or polished during the Muromachi Period. There were a number of great painters and architects at work as well as one of Japan's finest engravers; at the same time, the art of lacquer-work reached a height it has never attained since.

Everybody was a poet, and almost everybody was a Zen Buddhist. The various arts of the theatre were highly developed, as were both the tea ceremony and flower arrangement. It is not often that a country can boast a

47

"golden age" so many-splendored – and all this while clan fought clan in an attempt to wrest power from the Ashikaga.

At length the last Ashikaga shogun was replaced by Oda Nobunaga, one of the most imposing figures in Japanese history, for it was he who put an end to the civil wars that had been depleting the country and who began the necessary work of reconstruction. He was also, incidentally, one of the few Japanese of importance before the Meiji restoration who realized that Japan's continued policy of strict isolation was of more harm than help to the progress of the country. It is interesting to speculate what Japan's history might have been had Nobunaga not been assassinated by one of his own generals at the early age of forty-eight.

He was replaced by an equally remarkable man, Toyotomi Hideyoshi, but one who reversed his predecessor's policy of interest in the great world outside – save for two rash and unsuccessful assaults on Korea. Yet Hideyoshi did continue Nobunaga's attempt to reunify and pacify the country, and by the time of his death, at sixty-two, when the Tokugawa made their successful bid for power, they found a firm foundation upon which to build. Their long and successful, though stringently controlled, reign could not have been successful without the work of their two extraordinary predecessors.

This brief pre-Tokugawa period, at the end of the sixteenth century, takes its name from the two castles of the remarkable men who dominated it. Azuchi Castle was built by Nobunaga, and Momoyama ·was the hill on which Hideyoshi built his own magnificent castle; the period, 'thus, is known as the Azuchi-Momoyama and was no less distinguished than the years that preceded it for its contribution to Japanese culture. All of the arts and ceremonies flourished, and one in particular had its first faint beginnings when a well-disposed young lady tried to raise money for her shrine by giving a charity matinee. Soon other performers were added to the production, which took the name of kabuki and became Japan's major theatrical art. Tokyo, even today, has two huge theatres largely given over to kabuki productions. One, the Kabuki-za, was first built in 1660.

The Tokugawa shogunate began with Ieyasu, who successfully defeated his rivals in the famous battle of Sekigahara and established his *bakufu* in Edo (now Tokyo). It was during the Tokugawa (or Edo) Period that Japan's caste system became so rigidly codified, with the court nobles at the top, followed by the warriors, the farmers, and the townsfolk (or merchants). The nobles, however, despite their social eminence, wielded little or no real power: that was in the hands of the feudal lords, or dai-myo, who divided the country into fiefs, which they ruled under the exalted power of the Tokugawa shogun in Edo. This dual system so confused the rest of the world, when it tried to make contact with Japan, that the word *taikun* (tycoon) was applied indiscriminately to both the Emperor in Kyoto and the shogun in Edo, although within Japan it was used to refer exclusively to the shogun. President Buchanan, for instance, spoke of "His Imperial Majesty the Tycoon." (The word itself means merely "great prince" and could not possibly be used to describe the august Mikado.)

During the beginning of Ieyasu's shogunate, in the early seventeenth century, foreigners first began to call at Japanese ports in their sailing vessels, traders and missionaries alike, and at first they were welcomed. At the same time, Japanese ships now began to sail to nearby Asian ports; Ieyasu even undertook the daring adventure of sending commercial representatives all the way across the Pacific to New Spain, as Mexico was then called. Ieyasu followed the policy of his predecessor, Hideyoshi, of prohibiting Christianity, but did not enforce the prohibition very strictly, and a number of missionaries (largely Jesuits) came to Japan in an effort to persuade its people that only strict adherence to the tenets of the two Testaments would enable them to enter

Heaven. Fortunately or not (depending on one's point of view), Iemitsu, the third Tokugawa shogun, prohibited Christianity absolutely – with the result that modern-day Japanese are free of the burden of guilt that the Judeo-Christian philosophy tends to impose. Fortunately or not, Iemitsu also forbade Japanese to leave the country or to return once they had left. For more than two centuries Japan was now almost totally isolated from the rest of the world.

One result of this policy was that Japan was now able to develop her arts free from outside influence. The stupendous efforts that Western painters were making to master the laws of perspective and achieve the illusion of a third dimension in a two-dimensional art had no effect on Japanese painters. As a result, they developed a skill in the use of line and color that, when their works finally reached Europe in the late nineteenth century, astounded the Impressionists and had a profound effect on the future of Western painting.

This influence began in quite a haphazard way – and occurred as a result of the adamant insistence of the Western powers in engaging in trade with the island empire. Commodore Perry was the first to overcome Japanese resistance. He concluded an American-Japanese treaty in 1854, and soon thereafter other Western powers signed similar treaties. Japanese prints were so common and so cheap that the Japanese used them as wrapping paper for more precious objects – and it was in this wholly fortuitous manner that the prints found their way to the West and initiated an interest in Japanese art that, except during the years of the Pacific War, has steadily increased.

Relations were not always easy. There was a strong anti-foreign element in the country that wanted to see the Japanese ports closed again, and in 1867 this antagonism took as its spearhead the fifteen-year-old boy who ascended the throne as emperor with the posthumous name of Meiji. Since the shogun had proven himself unequal to the task of keeping Japan pure and

free from foreign influence, the isolationist
faction rallied around the new emperor and
succeeded in forcing the last Tokugawa shogun
to abdicate. Power was once again in imperial
hands. But if the isolationists supposed that
Meiji would put an end to Japanese communi-
cation with the world, they were doomed to
disappointment. The young emperor had other
and wiser advisers who realized that if Japan
was to take her rightful place among the great
powers, she would have to adopt the tactics of
the great powers: she would have to use their
science and technology, she would have to
reform her economy, she would have to trans-
form herself — in a word — from a feudal state
to an industrial state, and she would have to do
it as quickly and efficiently as possible. In this,
as events of the past century have proven, the
Emperor's advisors were undoubtedly right:
Japan's industrial and political eminence,
in this year of 1977, is no longer open to
question.

And yet with it all, Japan has retained her

own personality: it was not in her nature to become a mere stereotyped copy of a Western state. The way was often a thorny one; the country that for so many centuries had disdained the world was not always able to adapt herself successfully to the world's ways; and in her helter-skelter borrowing, she made many mistakes – but it was never long before she rectified them, and the corrections became part of the Japanese framework. A crucial first decision of Meiji and his advisers was to move his capital away from tradition-ridden Kyoto to the more vital city of Edo, the name of which was now changed to Tokyo – the Eastern Capital. (The character *kyo*, which appears in both names, means merely the capital city.)

It would be impossible, in so brief a summary as this, to list the many reforms that the new government undertook – from schools and the monetary system to the establishment of all sorts of factories and public banks to finance them. The government soon found that it was ill-equipped to manage the many factories that it had established and so it sold them – at greatly reduced prices – to private entrepreneurs: this was the beginning of the *zaibatsu,* the great industrial combines that ruled Japanese enterprise for so many years. They continued to maintain their special relation with the government, and it was often difficult to determine when one of the *zaibatsu* was acting on its own behalf and when it was acting on behalf of the government. During the pre-War years, the Imperial Army became the most powerful force in the government, and the *zaibatsu* maintained the same special relations with the Army that they had formerly enjoyed with a civil government. During the occupation, after the War was lost, the *zaibatsu* were dissolved by the Allied Powers, since which time they have tended to regroup – though without their former centralization. The many companies that compose what was formerly called the *zaibatsu* are now members of the Tokyo Stock Exchange and have millions of shareholders, many of them quite large, instead of a few family-owners, as before.

But we have got ahead of our story. The fact remains that the Meiji reforms were so immediately successful that by 1904 Japan was ready to wage a major war against a major Western power (Russia) and to win it — although she did not, at least in Japanese eyes, win the peace that followed. For this Japan tended to blame President Theodore Roosevelt, who mediated the Treaty of Portsmouth in 1905. It became one of the causes for Japanese antagonism toward the United States and its president, another Roosevelt, some three decades later.

One Meiji reform that had a profound effect on Japanese social life was the dissolution of the caste system (although vestiges of it persisted for many years), with the consequent insistence that all Japanese take a family name—a prerogative that had thitherto been reserved for the nobles.

With the so-called Manchurian Incident of 1932, Japan took over control of Manchuria and began extending her hegemony in mainland Asia. It was in this process that the Imperial Army acquired its extraordinary powers within Japan herself; civil cabinets became mere expressions of the will of the Army; members of the government who resisted the Army were forced into retirement or, if they continued to resist, were assassinated; and even the emperor found it difficult to withstand the growing military might. Meiji's son Taisho ascended the throne in 1912, and in 1926 the present Emperor acceded to power – but the power was, for a time, merely nominal.

There seems to be no question that the Emperor was opposed to the Army's growing insistence on confrontation with the United States, but he was unable to impose his will on a cabinet dominated by the Army, while at the same time President Roosevelt's intransigence did little to avert the impending catastrophe.

Anyone who wants to understand why Japan found herself declaring a war that very few knowledgeable Japanese believed she could win must take into account the peculiarly national distaste for individual decision-making and acceptance of responsibility. These are qualities that any foreign businessman sees in operation (sometimes to his despair) in Japan today, and they combined, from the Japanese point of view, to make war inevitable -- even though it was recognized that that war might well prove catastrophic. The Japanese do not favor the idea that one man can make a binding decision; they prefer that somehow or other a consensus be arrived at. And no man relishes accepting responsibility for a decision. That is why, once it was clear that the War was lost, only the Emperor, who is traditionally free of responsibility, was able to accomplish a peaceful surrender and avert a civil war that might have meant the end of the country. Even then, there was doubt, at the very last moment, that he would succeed -- for many Army officers believed that he was being "misled" by "traitorous" advisers and they were ready -- by force of arms if necessary -- to show him the right path. That they failed is Japan's -- and the world's -- good fortune.

Also fortunate all around was the fact that the American occupation was as benign and thoughtful as any military occupation could be. Its purpose was to extirpate any remaining vestige of the authority of the Imperial Army and to make Japan a democratic state. The reforms were extensive: the *zaibatsu*, as we have already noted, were dissolved (although, in line with Japanese economic policy, they have tended to regroup); many great land-holdings were broken up, and the land was distributed among people who had formerly been merely tenant-farmers; the Emperor renounced the divinity that had been conferred on him by myth and concurred in for centuries by his subjects. He became a constitutional monarch, and the constitution ensured universal free elections, with an upper and a lower house somewhat similar to the Senate and the House of Representatives in the United States. Most extraordinary of all, perhaps, in an occupation headed by a military commander was the fact that Japan in her new constitution renounced war as a means of settlement of international disputes. The armed forces of Japan at present consist merely of a token Self-Defense Force. For the fact that such extensive reforms, some of which touched the innermost fiber of national life, were carried out with a minimum of oppression and humiliation, General Mac-Arthur must be given a large share of credit.

Japan regained her independence in 1952, and in 1956 became a member of the United Nations, where she has played an increasingly vital role. Her economic recovery, which has been the wonder and envy of the rest of the world, contributed largely of course to her renewed prestige in international life. At no previous time in Japanese history has she held so strategic a position in world affairs.

Perhaps a word or two about the present-day Japanese government might be helpful. As we have already noted, the Emperor renounced his divinity and became instead a symbol of the State; from the constitutional point of view, the important aspect of this revolutionary change was the fact that sovereignty no longer rested with the Emperor but rather with all of the people. In some ways their sovereignty is greater than that of the American people, and the rights guaranteed them by their Constitution are more sweeping than those guaranteed by the Constitution of the United States.

For instance, although the new Constitution recognizes the independence of the legislative, executive, and judicial branches, as in the United States, the Japanese people not only elect members of the legislative body, the National Diet, but the executive organ, the Cabinet, is responsible to the Diet. It is headed by the prime minister, the head of the majority party, who appoints its sixteen members, all of whom must be civilians and at least half of whom must be elected members of the Diet. The judicial system, headed by the Supreme Court, is also more directly controlled by the elected representatives of the people than in many other countries. The chief justice of the Supreme Court is appointed by the Emperor after being designated by the cabinet; the other fourteen judges are appointed by the cabinet but are subject to popular examination at general elections that follow their appointment. Further, they are subjected to a similar examination every ten years. Lower court justices are similarly appointed and controlled. Thus the voice of the people may be heard directly in all three branches of government — a situation that Americans might, in some instances, find enviable, for it would be impossible for Japan to have an "unpopular" justice of the Supreme Court: he would very likely not be appointed, and if he were appointed he would not be approved by the people.

The ruling party is a conservative one, the Liberal-Democrats: they control both the lower body of the Diet (the House of Representatives) and the upper body (the House of Councillors). The term of office for the former is four years, for the latter six years, but if the Diet is dissolved, then the Representatives lose their membership in the House and a new election must take place. The Diet must be dissolved, or the cabinet must resign *en bloc,* if the Diet passes a vote of no-confidence against the cabinet or if the Diet rejects a vote of confidence by the cabinet. Members of the House of Councillors are elected for a term of six years, half of them every three years. The upper body cannot be dissolved, but if the House of Representatives is dissolved, then the Councillors adjourn until after the House of Representatives reconvenes with its newly-elected members. Suffrage is universal for all Japanese citizens, male or female, over twenty years of age.

To a large extent, Japan is a welfare state, with compulsory education, health insurance, provisions for old age and retirement. Aside from the various ministries whose heads are members of the cabinet, the Prime Minister's Office has under its jurisdiction such organizations as the Bureau of Pensions, the Fair Trade Commission, the National Public Safety Commission, the Economic Planning Agency, and the like. In such matters, as well as in the efficiency of its public service, not to mention the vitality of its private enterprise, Japan is more like one of the Scandinavian countries than like any other country in Asia. (The foreigner will be interested to learn that the Tokyo Metropolitan Police Department has a special telephone number for foreigners who get in trouble or who require help. We hope you won't need the number, and probably you won't, but if you do, it's 581-4321; the man who answers will almost certainly speak English and probably some other language as well.)

We have already commented, as has just about everybody else who has written about Japan in the last two decades, on the country's economic resurgence, but a few details might be helpful in understanding just how tremendous and remarkable this has been. The actual rate of growth in recent years has averaged around 17% and has been reflected in almost all aspects of the economic life of the country, from heavy industry, petrochemicals, and electronics to the now controversial textiles as well as agriculture and fisheries. There is virtually no sphere where Japanese industry has not shown itself both aggressive and progressive – sometimes to the detriment even of its friends. Japan, for instance, now exports far more to the United States than she imports, and this unfavorable (from the American point of view) balance of trade has been receiving attention from both government and industry.

Japan must, of course, continue to expand her export trade in order to be able to import the many natural resources she requires to feed her growing industries. The country depends very heavily on external sources – it was this fact, if no other, that made many people in both business and government realize that Japan, when she entered upon a war with the United States, was doomed to defeat. In fact, one of the men closest to the Emperor advised him as early as 1942, with the fall of Singapore, that there could be no more favorable time for the government to seek peace, for the scarcity of such strategic materials as iron, oil, and rubber and the necessity to transport them considerable distances must in the end spell defeat. But the Emperor's government, effectively in the hands of the army, was unable to make a move toward peace; the war dragged on its sad and weary pace.

But happily all that is past. Japan is first among the countries of the world in shipping and shipbuilding, and that enables her to transport the materials she needs. Her present-day entrepreneurs are extremely ingenious in seeking out sources of raw material and, where necessary, supplying funds to exploit them. There are few countries in the world where Japanese agents are not busily engaged in prospecting and arranging for the purchase of material. Quite often this activity takes the form of a joint venture, where a Japanese company invests the major share of capital required and divides the produce with a native country: this, of course, is most common in underdeveloped countries which lack the necessary funds themselves.

As a result, Japan, since the end of the War, has become industrialized at an unheard-of tempo, not only in shipping but in other forms of transportation – no other country in the world, for instance, can equal the "bullet train" that plies at half-hour intervals between Tokyo and Osaka. It does the 325 miles in three hours and ten minutes! And it does them comfortably too. (Long Island commuters, take note.) The merger between Yawata and Fuji has made the combined company the second largest steel-producer in the world, exceeded only by United States Steel. As for electronics, it seems doubtful that there is any country in the world now that is unfamiliar with the products of Sony, Matsushita, and the many lesser manufacturers. It is astonishing to realize that all this has been accomplished in a country that is virtually devoid of raw material – and has been accomplished in a few short years.

As for Japanese farming, it must necessarily be on a small scale as compared with that of other countries possessing far greater arable land areas. The average farmer works less than a couple of acres, and the rate of increase of his income during the post-war years compares unfavorably with that of industrial workers. For that reason, many farmers prefer to give up their land entirely and switch over to industry or to engage in secondary occupations in order to increase their income. It has been estimated that about seventy per-cent of Japanese farmers do non-agricultural work, leaving the planting of the rice, say, to their wives and children. Despite development programs and government subsidies, farmers' incomes still lag behind those of the nation as a whole.

This might be a good place to say a word about the apparent fact that Japanese salaries are so much lower than those of workers in other highly industrialized countries. The fact is, however, less real than apparent. Although wages and salaries are indeed low, every employee of a Japanese company is entitled to fringe benefits that are often worth more than his salary itself. Such benefits may range all the way from free housing to well-nigh inexhaustible expense accounts that enable a highly-placed employee to entertain customers at geisha houses — one of the most expensive and — to the visitor, at least — one of the most boring forms of entertainment on earth. Sometimes the company may pay for free vacation trips, sometimes it will pay the employee's taxes; both severance pay and retirement pay tend to be high. Advancement in most Japanese companies is on the basis of seniority rather than merit, and a company seldom fires an employee except for the grossest infringements of duties. All companies pay at least one bonus a year (around Christmas time) and most pay two (in June and December). These vestiges of feudalism mean that Japan's economic system is wholly unlike that of the West, which places so high a value on mobility — but however "backward" Japan may be, the system has worked miraculously well, and the worker himself, considering all the benefits he receives in addition to his basic salary, is no worse off than his counterpart in the West, and often it will be found that he is in reality better off.

Of course Japan's economy is beset by many of the problems that presently plague the West. The encroachment of automation means that fewer workers are needed, and labor unions are constantly complaining – although at the same time Japanese managers complain that there is a shortage of labor! Probably the explanation is a simple one that is familiar in many other countries: the shortage is of skilled labor, while the men who are being replaced by machines are unskilled. Although education is compulsory in Japan, many children do not go beyond the lower secondary school, with the result that they are not equipped to perform the highly skilled work that a highly industrialized society requires.

Nonetheless, whether they are equipped to

get a good job or not, the young, boys and girls both, flock to the big cities, all of which are by now overcrowded. Housing in all the large cities is at a premium, with Tokyo taking pride of place. As foreign residents learn to their sorrow, rents for what Americans would call medium-sized apartments are outrageously high, even by American standards. In Japan, these apartments are all "super de luxe" and the apartment houses are usually called "mansions."

Traffic congestion in and around the large cities, as more and more automobiles roll off the assembly lines, is becoming an increasingly difficult problem. Tokyo is not only the world's largest city insofar as population goes, but it also occupies an enormous area -- so the problem of getting from one end of it to the other can be an extremely vexatious one. The city is constantly adding to its network of elevated express highways, but the added highways hardly keep pace with the ever-growing population and its need to get from one place to another. Tokyo is being (temporarily, at least) saved by its extremely efficient subway system -- but here again more subway lines are needed, and the difficulty of tunneling under existing dwellings is a familiar one in large cities all over the world. Other familiar problems are air and water pollution, of which Tokyo is no freer than any other great capital.

Among the most remarkable changes that have occurred in the past century is the fact that Japan, once the most isolated country of Asia, is now the most dominant in international affairs. The role that might, in the 1970's, have been played by China is being increasingly delegated to Japan, in part because of Communist China's own xenophobia and in part because of most of the rest of the world's sinophobia.

It is not only in the formation of joint ventures for the exploitation of natural resources that Japan is playing an ever more crucial role in the less developed countries of Southeast Asia but she is also offering aid and technical training on an expanding basis in addition to the hundreds of millions of yen and the hundreds of millions of yen worth of goods that she has paid and is paying in the form of reparations as a result of the Pacific War. As the most prosperous country of Asia, Japan realizes that it is to her own advantage to increase the prosperity of her neighbors. Further, the economic and political stability of Southeast Asia is directly dependent on the prosperity of its people. Japan, having renounced war, is keenly interested in this problem — not only in Southeast Asia, where she is a dominant force, but in the rest of the world as well, where her prestige and economic power enable her to exert an ever growing influence in the peaceful settlement of differences between the "two worlds."

She maintains good relations with a number of communist states and has entered upon several joint ventures with the Soviet Union for the exploitation of natural resources in Siberia, although the United States is, of course, the country with which her economic ties are strongest. It has been estimated that there are now in existence over seven hundred Japanese-American joint-venture companies, and the exchange of technical know-how is constant.

Not all is roses, of course, as anybody knows who reads the daily newspaper. Competition is sometimes sharp, and there are differences of opinion on the two sides of the Pacific as to how things ought to be done. The Japanese want to "liberalize" their industry slowly, so as to avoid that most dreaded of Japanese bugbears -- disruption of harmony; Americans, on the other hand, would rather see things done yesterday than tomorrow. The result, inevitably, is a frayed nerve or two on one side or the other -- but perhaps as extraordinary as any other post-War phenomenon is how well the two countries have contrived to work together, considering what one might have thought would be insuperable differences in national temperament. Perhaps it's the differences that permitted the collaboration to work!

3. CUSTOMS

CUSTOMS

Are you bristling with letters of introduction to Japanese and Western acquaintances and business associates in Japan? The Japanese you look up will assuredly be pleased to see you, for in that sense, they are the Greeks of the Orient: they like visitors. In all likelihood — be prepared to be disappointed — the Japanese you look up will take you out to a restaurant rather than invite you home. Later, after you get to know one another, you may be asked to visit them in their houses, and in that case you will want to know what to expect. Your local Western introductions will be freer with invitations home, but you'll probably find that they've long since taken to some Japanese ways and that their houses are more Japanese than Western. So many of the same rules apply.

The first, of course, is one you know already: it's better with your shoes off. All Japanese residences, whether they are pretty little wooden houses with sloping roofs or apartments in large, often monstrous ferro-

concrete buildings, have an entrance-way just inside the front door where you are expected to remove your shoes. Very likely there will be a maid waiting to help you, to store your shoes away and offer you a pair of house slippers as you step inside. You may prefer, as many Japanese do, to dispense with the slippers and go around in your stocking feet. The latter custom, however hard it may be on the stockings, is awfully comfortable – and once you get used to it, you'll probably wonder why you ever bothered to wear shoes in your own house back home.

"A place for everything, and everything in its place" is not a Japanese saying. Because of the nature of their houses, the architecture and the furnishings, almost any room can be used for almost any purpose. Rooms in Japanese houses are usually divided not by hard and fast walls but by easily removable sliding paper doors. Many Japanese sleep on foam rubber or plastic mattresses that are laid out on the floor at night and stored out of sight during the day,

CUSTOMS

— in the evening —

— at night —

so there is no reason a bedroom should not be used as a dining room, or vice versa. This interchange is rendered particularly easy by the fact that Japanese like to sit on cushions on the floor and eat at low tables. At least one room in the average Japanese dwelling has flooring of *tatami* (rush mats), and here etiquette demands that you leave even your house slippers behind.

Of course customs in Japan are changing, as they are everywhere else in the world, and now affluent Japanese households have at least one Western room, with carpets and real Western furniture -- or rather, with what the Japanese fondly suppose to be real Western furniture. There's a difference! In the fashioning of traditional objects, Japanese taste is famous -- but all too often, when the Japanese imitate unfamiliar Western objects, the taste is likelier to be infamous. If you have any doubts about this, wander through the house-furnishings floor of one of the large department stores.

You will probably want to buy some of the things you see only because they are so outrageous — and you will probably resist. preferring to put your money in some lovely old (or modern) bowl of traditional design or in a length of hand-dyed cloth or in a chest-of-drawers a couple of hundred years old with lines as clean as the most austere Scandinavian designer could hope to achieve.

And these, incidentally, are among the things you will see, if you are lucky, when you pay your initial visit to a Japanese household. One other feature that is almost universal in Japan is the *tokonoma* — a good-sized recess in one wall where the master of the house hangs one of his favorite scrolls, perhaps a painting, perhaps some calligraphy, and where some other member of the household (at least one of them is sure to have studied *ikebana*) has added a seasonal flower arrangement. The flowers, naturally, have to be changed fairly often; the scroll is usually replaced when the master or mistress of the household decides it has got so familiar no one is looking at it any more. This feature — the changing about of exhibits – is characteristic also of Japanese museums, most of which have so many scrolls they cannot possibly display them all, so that only someone who lives all his life in Japan and makes a habit of frequenting its many museums regularly can hope to see the whole wealth of painting and calligraphy that Japan possesses. A visitor who wants to see a particular object in a particular museum would be well-advised to come armed with potent letters of introduction, so if the object is not on display, the director of the museum will be persuaded to have it brought out.

When Japanese visit each other, particularly if the time of day calls for it, they are often invited first of all to have a bath. You, as a foreigner, may not be so favored – the reason being that the Japanese, easily embarrassed themselves, would not want to invite you to do something you are almost certain to do wrong.

A family bath is likely to be made of wood, much higher and much shorter than Western baths, with a wooden cover that makes it easier to heat the water, retain the heat, and keep the water clean. For the water, customarily, is not only not changed for every member of the household, as it usually is in the West, but it is not changed every day. And that is where the Japanese are afraid you will go wrong for they know that you customarily get into a tubfull of hot water and then soap yourself, while they do all their soaping and rinsing outside the tub and climb into it only to luxuriate, in water so hot most Westerners find it painful rather than pleasurable.

Should you happen to go to a public bath, of which there are thousands all over the country, the same procedure applies. You are expected to be as clean as possible *before* you enter the bath to soak along with half-a-dozen or a dozen other people. Generally there is a partition between the men's bath and the women's bath, but this distinction is not always made, particularly in hot springs resorts where people go expressly for the supposed medicinal properties of the water. As one doctor said on the subject of hot springs, the chances are very high that the water won't hurt you.

Well, let us suppose you have successfully navigated the *genkan* (where you have left your shoes), admired the *tokonoma*, and taken your bath with due regard for the proprieties. You will now be invited to partake of some food and drink -- but the invitation in Japan is a strange one, for Japan is still as formal a country as America is not. No "Come and get it!" here, not even "Dinner is served, madam." Your Japanese host, following tradition, may well remark as he indicates a laden table, "There is nothing to eat but I hope you will eat it anyway." Your temptation will be to reply, "Who you kidding, mac?" Resist it. Smile and bow; fold yourself under the table in any way that seems most comfortable to you, or at any rate least uncomfortable; and try the strange, beautifully arranged foods that the household has been working all day to prepare for you. Probably there will be no knives and forks –

only chopsticks and probably some of the foods will taste too strange to be palatable; but very likely your Japanese hosts will have made an effort to compromise Japanese with Western cooking and some dishes you will find down-right delicious. In any case, they have made their effort; now you must make yours. And by the time you have finished, you will have drunk enough saké to say, "Gochiso-sama deshita" ("It was indeed delicious"), at which your host, whose face will have grown flushed with saké, will compliment you on your excellent Japanese. All in all, a pleasant evening – not nearly as bad as you, and your Japanese host, feared.

But most of your eating in Japan, as we have already noted, will probably be done in restaurants – and Japan boasts a great variety of them, both Oriental and Western. Smaller, and cheaper, restaurants are likely to have a kind of showcase outside, with one shelf, or several, with plates containing wax imitations of the various dishes that the restaurant features, each with a price tag. The Japanese are remarkably clever at fabricating "wax food," whether it be a simple curried rice or a breaded pork chop or an ice-cream sundae. The system, which is intended to attract Japanese clients, works well for the foreigner who speaks no Japanese and who wants to sample the humbler eating houses, since all he has to do is summon a waiter or waitress outside and point to what he wants. What he gets will be virtually indistinguishable from the display — except that it won't be made of wax, it will be made of food. Main dishes in restaurants of this sort usually cost between fifty cents and a dollar.

But the food is not of the gourmet variety, nor is it even "typically" Japanese — it is simply what the busy, not very affluent workingman or (to use a Japanese word) salaryman fills his belly with when he can't get home to eat. Portions are not, by Western standards, very large, for the Japanese, a small, slender people, tend to eat sparingly. Overweight Japanese are the exception — not, like Americans, the rule.

Most likely eating in one of Japan's little neighborhood restaurants will be an occasional adventure; most of your eating will be done in Western-style restaurants, of which all of Japan's larger cities boast a wide variety -- French, Italian, German, Spanish, even Mexican. Prices here tend to be much higher, of course, and menus are usually printed in English and perhaps some other foreign language as well as Japanese, so you will have no trouble ordering. Your hotel, too, will have a variety of restaurants if you don't feel like going out. Your bill will include, in addition to the food you've eaten, a government tax and a service charge, so tipping is not expected unless you have demanded some special service that you think ought to be rewarded. The same is true, by the way, of Japan's taxicabs.

You must not forget, when you think about where to eat, that there are plenty of Oriental restaurants to choose from – Indian and various kinds of Chinese foods as well as spe-

cialized Japanese restaurants. Of the latter, some are famous for their sukiyaki, others for their tempura (where the food is dipped in batter and deep-fried). Some connoisseurs claim that Japanese beef is the best in the world; the finest is usually called Kobe beef or Matsuzaka, and although it costs the earth (as well as the beer the cattle are gorged with), you will certainly want to try it at least once.

There are a number of Japanese sweets, but foreigners usually don't take to them, nor to the strong-smelling dried fish the Japanese are so fond of. However, you will almost certainly like warm saké, and one of the best places to drink it is a *yakitori* restaurant, where they specialize in various kinds of barbecued fowl. There are two things to remember about saké. One is that you never pour out your own, unless of course you happen to be alone; if you are with friends, each pours saké for the other – usually into thimble-sized cups. Once everybody has had enough of these, this rule tends to relax. The other rule, however, is a rigid one: you must never drink saké with rice, for saké is distilled out of rice, and the Japanese consider rice on rice to be improper. Nor do they consider it proper to drink saké *after* you have eaten your rice; since, with many Japanese meals, rice is served at the end, this does not constitute a very serious hardship.

One type of Japanese restaurant we have not yet mentioned which usually finds favor with foreigners is that which specializes in *sushi*. There is an almost endless variety of *sushi*, which is basically a ball of slightly vinegared rice, sometimes wrapped in specially prepared seaweed. The variety comes in the raw fish that is laid across it. The greatest fish-eaters in the world, the Japanese are tremendously skilled in preparing it, and there is almost no fish that escapes their attention. Some restaurants, for instance, specialize in *fugu*, an unfriendly variety of blowfish that has to have its poison very carefully removed before it may be safely eaten. Fugu-preparers are licensed by law; one restaurant proprietor recently killed himself after a customer died of eating improperly prepared *fugu*. The Emperor, by the way, is not supposed to eat it – and you may feel that what's not good enough for him isn't good enough for you either. Japan, after all, is a democracy.

There are innumerable other Japanese dishes that might be mentioned, such as the many kinds of noodles that are so popular, particularly after a night of heavy drinking, or the bean pastes (*miso*) that the Japanese like to eat at breakfast and other odd times of the day and that Westerners seldom like to eat at all.

One art you will have to master, if you haven't already, is that of using chopsticks (*hashi*). It is no more difficult than using a knife and fork – but Westeners usually feel just as clumsy at first as Japanese do the first time they use a knife and fork. To help you in getting your master's degree in *hashi*, we append below a diagram showing how they're used.

A few tips might be helpful for the man who comes to do business in Japan, and of them all

CUSTOMS

HOW TO USE CHOPSTICKS

1. As shown in figure "A", hold first chopstick firm and stationary in fixed position.
2. As shown in figure "B", second chopstick is held like a pencil, with the tips of thumb, index and middle fingers. Manipulate this chopstick to meet the first chopstick.
3. As shown in figure "C", this manipulation will form "V" to pick up the food.

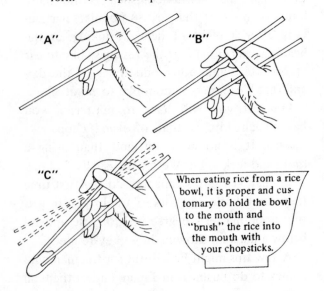

"A"   "B"

"C"

When eating rice from a rice bowl, it is proper and customary to hold the bowl to the mouth and "brush" the rice into the mouth with your chopsticks.

probably the most important is; don't try to be a ten-day wonder, solving in a few days problems your local representative hasn't been able to solve in a few months. All you'll do is mess things up for him. He'll lose face and authority in Japanese eyes -- and it will probably take him months to undo the damage you may do in a few hours. He knows far more about the local scene than you do. Trust his judgment − or find someone else whose judgment you do trust. You can have only the foggiest notion of how things are done in Japan -- but of one thing you may be sure: it's not the way things are done at home.

Above all, don't suppose that for that reason your way is better. Japan's economic progress gives abundant proof to the contrary, as does the fact that you've come with your hat in your hand.

Be sure to give your local office plenty of advance notice as to when you arrive, how long you plan to stay, whom you want to see, and what you hope to accomplish. The more advance notice they have, the easier your job will be. And once you've given them dates, don't change them: there's a chronic shortage of hotel rooms in Tokyo, and changing a reservation can be a full-time headache. Bear in mind that the better your hotel, the more respect you'll get from the Japanese you've come to do business with. Life will be expensive -- probably fifty dollars a day at least, including $20 or more for your hotel room and a similar amount for food and drink. Try to avoid any appointments your first few days – you'll need them to get acclimatized. But when you do make an appointment, or have one made for you, be punctual about keeping it.

Remember that you're a foreigner in an *insular* country, a country that has evolved its own ways of doing things and that makes a sharp distinction between its own citizens and the rest of the world. In Japan there are only two kinds of people: Japanese and foreigners. There are no shades of gray. So try to follow local customs – it's the only way you'll get anything accomplished. Don't do any backslapping and don't talk Madison Avenese. It will only lead to endless explanations, and the result will probably be a total lack of comprehension.

Most of the time you'll be talking to interpreters, whether you know it or not. Then, towards the end, if things are going well, you may meet someone in authority. Even if you do, you will find it extremely difficult to get a yes or no answer from him. Our earlier remarks about decision-making apply to business as well as government. There is virtually no majority decision in Japan: unless everybody in authority agrees, the deal is off -- or indefinitely postponed. Don't despair, however. You may decide that despite all the talk and tea nothing has been accomplished; then, a month after you return home, comes a letter with the decision that you'd been hoping for.

The language barrier is a formidable one. The Japanese are not good at foreign languages, and their own language is vague and complex.

The business letters they write in some alien tongue are likely to reflect the vagueness and complexity of their own language. You may find you need the help of a foreign resident to "translate" the letters. You will certainly need an interpreter, who may be supplied by the company you're in touch with; otherwise, you'll have to find your own. And unless you're prepared to waste a lot of time, you'll need a guide. There are few street names and no street addresses: people find their way by using a nearby landmark. You'll need a number of name cards, printed in English on one side and Japanese on the other; they're an essential to doing business in Japan, and you'll probably find you give out on the average of twenty a day. And receive twenty back. It's a good idea to make a note or two on each card, so you'll remember the man (and his company) and connect him with the name – for Japanese names will of course be strange and unfamiliar to you.

You'll be entertained – at parties in private rooms of restaurants or hotels, at hostess bars,

perhaps at geisha houses. As we have noted, Japanese tend to dress more formally than Westerners, so you will want to wear a dark suit when you go out with them – and when you go to business conferences too. No aloha shirts, please!

You may feel a lot of time is being wasted at these gatherings – but you'd be wrong, for the Japanese are sizing you up and coming to certain conclusions. Incidentally, your hosts probably won't be as drunk as they seem when the evening ends! If you are travelling with your wife, you must plan to leave her out of all such fun and games, except possibly a farewell party. Japanese wives almost never meet their husbands' foreign business acquaintances.

Presents are no great problem. You must accept those that are offered you, of course, and when you are home send thank-you notes and small gifts in return. After all, the exchange makes for good relations -- and comes off taxes on both sides.

There will be moments of frustration,

obviously. The Japanese time-sense is very different from yours, and so, as we have pointed out, is the Japanese way of arriving at a decision. Never let your feeling of frustration become apparent to your hosts, don't raise your voice, and never, *never* permit yourself to become obviously angry. The man who strikes the first blow – in Japan at least – loses the fight.

Incidentally, the language problem though a serious one, is not quite so tough as it seems. Four English-language daily newspaper, as well as a number of trade journals, are published in Tokyo and distributed throughout Japan, so you need never feel you have lost touch with the world. A little transistor radio will permit you to tune in on the United States Army's Far East Network, which gives news broadcasts on the hour around the clock, and at 6:55 p.m. six days a week the Japan Broadcasting Corporation gives five minutes of news in English.

Should you need a doctor, your hotel will have one available who speaks English, or you

CUSTOMS

can go to the Tokyo Medical Clinic (near Tokyo Tower, 9:30 a.m. to 5:00 p.m., weekdays), which has a staff of foreign doctors, all of whom speak English. Many of the medicines you may need are now manufactured in Japan, under foreign licenses, and in addition there is a pharmacy near the Ginza that specializes in imported drugs (at, alas, imported prices).

One last word. Don't be condescending. Don't suppose the Japanese are barbarians, yearning desperately for the light you are bringing them from the West. Bear in mind that you are lucky enough to be in one of the most civilized countries in the world. The rate of literacy in Japan is well-nigh 100%, and the Japanese read more newspapers and magazines (both foreign and domestic) than anybody else. They read books by their own authors, of course, one of whom won the 1968 Nobel Prize, but they read books by foreign writers too. There is no major work of Western literature that has not been translated into Japanese, the FM stations broadcast many hours of serious Western music every day, and shows of Western art are frequent and popular. Your Japanese host would blush if the thought were publicly expressed, but the fact is he probably knows as much about Western culture as you do, and quite possibly more. How much do you know about the culture of the East?

When in Japan, in the name of good manners, we beg of you, *don't*:

1. Wear shoes in a Japanese house.
2. Get soap in the bathwater.
3. Dress too conspicuously.
4. Raise your voice in anger.
5. Display loving emotion in public.
6. Be loud or raucous.
7. Ever ask a question in the negative form.
8. Be condescending.
9. Speak too rapidly.
10. Make love to your host's wife overtly.

4. THE ARTS AND⋯⋯

That the Japanese are among the most artistic people in the world has become a mere commonplace since the first *ukiyo-e* prints found their way to Europe and Europeans in turn began coming to Japan, where they found themselves bewildered by the variety of artistic expression -- and bewildered also by the fact that this expression was not confined to a relatively small group of artists and connoisseurs, as it generally is in the West, but rather was an integral part of the cultural life of the entire population. One has only to go to one of the many exhibitions arranged weekly by Japan's department stores, or attempt to penetrate the madding crowd that throngs a major exhibition of imported Western art (like the big Rembrandt show a couple of years back), or try to buy a seat for the Russian Ballet a mere week or two in advance, to realize that art is as popular with the Japanese as noodles.

They are most famous, perhaps, for their architecture, which has become a kind of symbol of the country -- whether it be the exuberance of Nikko or the magnificent austerity of the Katsura Imperial Villa at Kyoto. Since, until the Meiji restoration a hundred years ago, Japanese architects used wood almost exclusively, the rate of destruction by fire was inordinately high. However, the Japanese are a traditional people: when a shrine, a temple, or palace burnt down, it was replaced as soon as possible by an exact replica of the destroyed building. Thus, as one wanders about the country, looking at its sights, one can never be sure whether the building one is looking at was constructed a thousand years ago and refurbished yesterday or whether the entire construction dates from 1965.

And does it matter? The answer, in Japan, is that it matters very little indeed. There are no architects and sculptors living today who could replace the Cathedral at Chartres were it to be destroyed, but Japanese architecture has generally been distinguished for its simplicity and its regularity and harmony of line. That it sometimes attains greatness is due to these very qualities -- qualities that are, after all, as thoroughly within the grasp of present-day architects as they were a thousand years ago.

Much Japanese painting has also perished in the disastrous fires that have periodically ravaged the cities -- but like the architecture, much of it was immediately duplicated, and there is now a great wealth of painting in Japan's many museums. You may, after a few days of sightseeing, decide there is almost too much. Japanese painting was to a very large extent influenced by Chinese, and present-day museums and private collections are well-stocked with Chinese originals as well as Japanese derivatives not to mention a great mass of Korean material, paintings and books, brought to Japan as a result of the Hideyoshi invasion of Korea.

We do not propose to burden you with a discourse on the various schools of Japanese painting, their names, dates, characteristics, and chief exponents. If you are really interested in Oriental painting, then you probably know more than we do about the subject; otherwise, you will very likely go through a few museums and see some painted scrolls or screens that you like without caring very much when they were painted or by whom.

We used the expression "*ukiyo-e* prints" a while back, and perhaps a word of explanation is in order – since if you go to any of the large museums, you will be seeing a great many of the prints, and the familiar names of Hokusai and Hiroshige will be popping out at you from every corner. *Ukiyo-e* means, literally, "floating-world painting," and although print-making goes far back in Japanese art, *ukiyo-e* did not become popular until the Edo Period, when the townsfolk and common people wanted, and were able to pay for, prints of famous actors, beautiful women, and land- and townscapes. The prints were called floating-world paintings, presumably, to indicate that they were light in tone and evanescent and to distinguish them from the serious paintings of the "permanent world" of Kyoto.

Sculpture probably fared better than its sister fine arts, since both bronze and stone are more impervious to devouring tongues of flame. A number of ancient wooden statues have, however, survived and are usually to be seen in the temples, although a few have found their way to museums and private collections. Old Japanese sculptures are, almost without exception, images associated with Buddhism or Shinto, the former being by far the more popular with sculptors. The two monumental bronzes that have survived are the Great Buddhas at Nara and Kamakura; the Great Buddha of Kyoto is a wooden image almost sixty feet tall dating from the end of the sixteenth century, when it was carved to replace an older, and even taller, image that had been destroyed in an earthquake.

One fine art that makes a strong appeal to the Japanese and almost none at all to the Westerner, is calligraphy. In fact, the Japanese rate it no less high than painting, and it is no uncommon sight to see a Japanese stand for

five or ten minutes in a museum studying a
written scroll he considers to be particularly
beautiful. The Westerner will probably not
even slow his pace. There are a number of
schools in the present day that teach calligraphy, and there are annual competitions with
prizes for the winners and long newspaper dis-
sertations on the winning entries.

Certain crafts -- such as pottery, lacquer-
ware, woodcarving, and metalwork -- have been
elevated almost to the status of a fine art. Exhibitions of good examples of these crafts are
frequent. Department stores, as we have noted,
often arrange such shows; and private collections are likely to concentrate during a month-
long show on one particular article or period.
Japan is full of private collections which are
usually open to the public six days a week and
which generally make a small charge. Much the
same is true of public museums.

The Westerner making his first visit to Japan
will be surprised to learn that museums do not
have permanent exhibitions. A New Yorker

who could find his way blindfolded to a particular Rembrandt in the Metropolitan Museum will probably feel a little uneasy to learn that only a small fraction of the paintings possessed by the Tokyo National Museum are on display at any one time. A scroll that was there today may be gone tomorrow, and this is true of virtually all Japanese museums and private collections, although not of temple or shrine repositories. The latter sometimes display their treasures only once a year, and some particularly sacred image may never be shown. No one has ever seen the miraculous golden image of the Goddess of Mercy that is said to be enshrined in her temple in Tokyo.

You may want to try reading some translations of Japanese poetry or fiction, but it is not, in all truth, a language that translates easily or well into Western languages. There are, of course, exceptions -- but it will usually be found that the exceptions have gone rather a long way from the originals. Arthur Waley's translation of Lady Murasaki's "Tale of Genji" is a work of art in itself, rather like Fitzgerald's "Rubaiyat." Strangely enough, some Japanese say they would rather read Waley's translation than Lady Murasaki's original -- if only because the modern English is easier than the tenth-century Japanese. The book has also been translated into modern Japanese.

Thus, when you go to see a Noh or Kabuki play, you will be at no more of a loss than the Japanese sitting next to you -- except that he may already have seen the play half a dozen times and know it almost by heart. Otherwise, he will require a program that tells the story, scene by scene, in modern Japanese -- just as you will need one that tells it in English. Both, you will find, are available in the lobby -- as well as various kinds of refreshment, from fruit and ice cream to serious food and drink, for kabuki plays tend to go on for quite a long time. Some, in fact, are so long they have to be given at two separate performances of perhaps five hours each. The Japanese, mercifully endowed by their creator with adequate *sitzflei-*

sch, think this is just fine; you may find an hour or two sufficient, even though what is going on onstage is dramatic and colorful and imaginatively staged.

Noh is far older than kabuki – and (it follows) far harder to understand. It is also much less popular than kabuki – it is austere rather than theatrical, poetic and philosophical rather than bloodcurdling, and wholly incomprehensible unless you happen to have majored in ancient Japanese. This does not prevent it from being an experience you will probably not want to miss, although you will probably decide that once is enough, while kabuki has a kind of wild, attractive exuberance about it that may not put it on a par with peanuts and sex but that nonetheless draws the foreigner back a second or a third time and that ensures kabuki a place in his memories of Japan long after he has returned home.

First, a word about noh. It derives from various Buddhist entertainments that began to be imported from China as early as the seventh century, but it did not assume its present form until the time of Kan-ami and Ze-ami (in the fourteenth and fifteenth centuries). The latter was not only the most distinguished performer of his day but he was also the author of most of the two hundred noh plays in the present-day repertoire. In its solemn austerity, a noh play may be likened to an early drama by Aeschylus – while kabuki approaches the blood-and-thunder of Elizabethan drama.

As we noted earlier, kabuki came into being in the early seventeenth century when a maiden decided to raise funds for her shrine by dancing in public. The fact that she, and later her troupe, wore original, highly imaginative costumes is thought to account for the name, since the verb *kabuku* meant "to do something unusual or absurd." The girl's success inevitably invited imitators, who for some reason, were usually local prostitutes. Having no reputation to lose, these ladies began to perform in a manner that offended the stern Tokugawa Government, which responded by prohibiting the performance of kabuki dances by women. The only result this prohibition had was that the role of the prostitutes was now played by handsome young boys -- both onstage and off.

In fact, this substitution only reinforced a tendency that had long been perceptible among both the warriors and the monks. In 1653 the shogunate decided that a new law was necessary: they now decreed that only adult men could take part in a kabuki performance, using elaborate costumes and wigs to simulate both women and boys. It seems doubtful that the new law had any great effect on Japanese morality, but it did encourage kabuki to develop from its originally rather simple-minded one-scene sketch with dancing to the long, elaborate, highly theatrical plays that now attract full and enthusiastic houses whenever they are performed – which, in the larger cities, is most days of the year. The first performance usually begins around eleven in the morning.

All of the actors, following tradition, are men. Most of them, incidentally, are married and have children -- to whom they pass on their skill and art. It is extremely difficult for an outsider to enter the closed circle of kabuki families.

Another traditional form of theatrical entertainment is the kind of puppet play now called *bunraku*. The puppets are usually about two-thirds life-size and are manipulated not by strings but by three men wearing black veils. An expert and highly-regarded manipulator may be granted the right to perform without a veil as a mark of respect. The Japanese do not actually *see* these manipulators, and the foreign visitor, watching his first *bunraku* play, will find that he doesn't either. For one thing, the dolls are usually dressed in brightly colored clothes, while their manipulators wear black. For another, people all over the world have been accepting various theatrical conventions for thousands of years. A *bunraku* doll can be as persuasive as a deftly handled marionette.

While we are on the subject of the older arts, we might mention that from time to time there are concerts of ancient Japanese music performed (often by the orchestra of the Imperial Court) on ancient instruments. The Westerner will probably find the music novel rather than meaningful. The same is likely to be true of performances of ancient dancing. The protracted and ritualistic opening and shutting of a fan or a parasol that so delight a Japanese audience are likely to leave the Westerner not only unmoved but painfully bored.

It would be incorrect to give the impression that the only theatrical performances to be seen in Japan are ancient ones. A glance at the weekend newspaper will show that any number of modern plays are being performed all over Tokyo. Most authors are Japanese but many are foreign. In any case, however, save for occasional performances by amateur dramatic societies, the plays are all in Japanese -- so you will probably decide you can spend your time more profitably elsewhere, perhaps at one of the musical extravaganzas that represent Japan's determination to outgirl Radio City

Music Hall. Incidentally, all first-run movie houses in Japan show films in the original language, with Japanese subtitles; there's always a list in the daily newspapers.

We have not gone into a few other so-called arts that the Japanese are proud of and indeed passionately interested in. It is unlikely that you will want to take up the "art" of flower-arrangement, though your wife might like to go to a class or two if you have the time, and it is unlikely also that the long, slow ritual of the tea ceremony will fascinate you -- unless you happen to be a Zen Buddhist. There are also the so-called "martial arts" -- judo, karate, and the like -- which have millions of adherents in Japan and a number of schools and practice halls.

Other traditional Japanese sports, or arts if you insist, are fencing (*kendo*) and archery (*kyudo*). The latter is not very unlike its Western counterpart, but the former is much tougher than the elaborate duello developed in Europe from the Middle Ages onward.

By far the most popular of traditional Japanese sports is sumo -- and you will probably decide you ought to go at least once. After the first few matches, you will probably decide it's time to leave. Sumo wrestlers are the exceptions to the rule that the Japanese are almost never overweight; they are especially chosen and trained to be giants, fattened like Strasbourg geese until they weigh around two or three hundred pounds. The match itself may take only a few seconds -- but the preparations seem endless as two nearly naked giants enter the ring, bow to the audience, bow to each other, crouch, rise, crouch again, throw ceremonial salt into the ring, crouch, rise, and crouch again until at last the signal is given for the fight to start. Then the two mammoths tear into each other until any part of the body of one of them (save the feet of course) touches the ground or until one of the fighters is pushed out of the ring.

Certainly as popular as sumo, perhaps more so, are two Western sports that the Japanese took up in a big way after the end of the Pacific War: baseball and golf. Crack baseball players are among the highest paid performers in the country, while golf is looked on more as a status symbol, like color television. It is also vital to the country's economy: probably more deals are consumated on the golf links than around a conference table. That is why many companies pay for an employee's course of instruction as well as his entrance fee and membership in a highly-regarded golf club. The bowling alley is also a place where buyer meets seller – though the cost of the meeting is considerably less; buyer meets seller, that is, provided buyer has taken the precaution to reserve the use of an alley several days in advance.

Have we come a long way from the austere simplicity of Japanese architecture, with which this chapter began? We shall go one step further – to the garish, noisy pachinko parlor where (the visitor will soon decide) a hundred million Japanese spend most of their time. They don't, of course. If they did, how would they have accomplished their economic miracle? But the truth is the pachinko machine exerts a fascination for the Japanese that is equalled only by the fascination the one-armed bandit of Las Vegas has for the American. Neither the slot-machine nor the pachinko-machine stands idle for very long, and the proprietors of both are unlikely to be paupers.

The chief difference between the two is that pachinko requires a certain amount of skill, so that, in a sense, it is a kind of combination of slot machine and pin-ball machine. The player buys a number of small metal balls (that cost two yen each) and then stands in front of a small box and tries to shoot the ball into a hole that is protected by a ring of nails. If he succeeds, he is rewarded with a shower of more little metal balls which, when the fascination of the game has begun to pall, he may exchange for things like cigarettes, canned foods, and the like. Then, if he chooses, he goes around the corner (presumably he knows the neighborhood) to a shop that will accept the merchandise at a discount and give him money in return. This latter transaction is, perhaps, on the fringe of illegality.

Let us close the chapter with still another kind of parlor that is considered propitious for the transaction of business and also for the furtherance of harmony in the company. It is for the latter reason that many employers encourage their employees to have a night out together in a mah jong parlor. The cost of the use of the table, the tea, and the snacks is small, though the stakes may often be high -- far higher than the worker can afford. Yet presumably, even if he has to cut down on his lunches for a month or so, to make up for his losses, he feels no rancor against his fellow-workers and -players.

Since one thing has led so precipitously to another in this chapter, let us just mention here that if you are a wife whose husband is going to be spending a lot of time at business conferences and if you are a member of a duplicate bridge club back home, you will be welcomed

at the Tokyo Bridge Club, which often has two
sessions a day, at 1 p.m. and 6 p.m. Most of the
players will be Japanese, of course, and many
of them will not speak English, but they'll all
be bilingual bidders! And know the latest conventions.

5. SIGHTSEEING

SIGHTSEEING

One thing about Asian countries is that they refuse to make life easy for the sightseer. In the first place, there's the perennial language problem; in the second, you will encounter millions of Asians looking at the sights at the same time you do; in the third, sights in Asia *sprawl.* The tourist who feels at home in Europe, with its well-ordered churches and palaces, is in for a shock when he starts trying to "do" the sights of Asia. Even so small a country as Japan makes spatial demands on her visitors that sometimes seem entirely unreasonable – particularly on a hot, muggy summer afternoon.

Delusions of grandeur would seem to have been an endemic disease with Oriental architects for a good many centuries. Even so modest a man as Frank Lloyd Wright was infected with the virus when he designed the old Imperial Hotel in Tokyo, now demolished to make way for a more "modern" building that uses space more economically – and profitably. Old-time residents -- even those who regarded the old building as something of a monstrosity

– regret its absence but recognize that it failed to meet the demands of an overcrowded, still-growing city.

When a Westerner thinks of the word "temple," he is likely to picture in his mind's eye a building as spatially neat as, let's say, the Parthenon in Athens. A Buddhist "temple," however, is usually a vast compound, covering perhaps several acres, with numerous buildings and gardens and, wherever possible, fountains, ponds, and waterfalls.

Or take the Imperial Palace at Kyoto. It is enclosed by a wall nearly five hundred yards long and about two hundred and fifty yards wide. Within are several main buildings and a number of smaller ones as well as gardens of various kinds, streams, lakes, and so on. To get all the bad news over with at once, let us remind the visitor that once he has entered the precincts of a temple, shrine, or palace, the only method of locomotion available to him is what his grandfather called shanks' mare.

He can, of course, get as far as the entrance-way by motor, and very likely his best plan is to make use of the excellent tours arranged all over the country by the Japan Travel Bureau. We realize that there are a good many people who try to avoid organized tours as they would the plague, who want only to poke around on their own -- but they must be prepared to pay the price, not only in money, taxiing from one sight to another in a large city like Kyoto, where many of the main sights are on the outskirts of the city, can be remarkably expensive, but also in time and frustration. It is not, after all, the driver's job to plan your tour for you and take you from place to place by the shortest and quickest route. If you are admantly determined to avoid group sightseeing, hire a car, a chauffeur, and a guide – and be prepared to pay the price.

Let us return, somewhat more realistically, to the Japan Travel Bureau, which has been in the business of showing Japan to tourists since 1912. The Bureau has offices in all the large hotels, as well as scattered about the cities, and there is always someone who speaks a bit of English.

Just so we will not be accused of favoritism, we will mention forthwith that there is also a Japan Association of Travel Agents that cater to foreign tourists as well as a Japan Guide Association, whose members are licensed by the government. Whatever travel bureau you use, you will find that there is an English-speaking young lady aboard your bus whose job it is to keep talking. After a while, you may regret not having brought your wax ear-plugs.

Your first port of call in Japan will almost certainly be Tokyo, from which you will want to make excursions to Kamakura, Nikko, and perhaps Mt. Fuji if the weather permits. Then, if you have the time, you will want to head west to Nagoya, the center for visiting the great Ise Shrines, and on to Osaka and Kyoto, from which you may make a day's excursion to Nara. These are, so to speak, the basic sights. If you are blessed with time to spare, you might want to visit Japan's enchanting Inland Sea and

SIGHTSEEING

continue on to the southern island of Kyushu. Or you may opt for the North: Hokkaido, with its Ainu villages and still primitive life; or Tohoku, in Northeast Japan, which is still further off the beaten track. If you want to do any really hard-core sightseeing, you will probably want the excellent and extremely thorough guidebook compiled by the Japan National Tourist Organization. And you will want to make a note of the fact that the Organization maintains offices both in Tokyo and Kyoto as well as at the Tokyo Airport, all staffed with extremely knowledgeable young ladies who speak excellent English and who are prepared to answer just about any question you have. The Organization also maintains a telephone service in Tokyo to help foreigners with answers to hard questions. Call 502-1461 in English or French during office hours, 9:00 a.m. to 5:00 p.m.

There is not much left in modern-day Tokyo to remind the visitor that it is quite an old city, fortified in ancient times and known as Edo as long ago as the twelfth century. In 1603 it became the seat of the shogunate and so, in reality, the most important city in the country, although Kyoto was to remain the home of the emperors until 1868. During the War, much of what remained of the old city was destroyed by bombing, and since the end of the War reconstruction and repopulation have made Tokyo the largest city in the world, with an area of nearly eight hundred square miles and a population that is expected to exceed twelve million soon.

Yet there is plenty for the tourist to see and enough to keep him busy for just about as long as he wants to stay: some tourists who had planned only a few weeks' visit find themselves spending the rest of their lives there. Not, we hasten to add, that the city is a beautiful one – but it is busy and exciting and vital, and nowhere else in the world will the visitor find a mammoth city whose residents are so kind, so easy to get on with, and so very, very patient with people who don't speak a word of their

SIGHTSEEING

language. One has only to think of Parisians, say, or New Yorkers, to realize how different Tokyoites are.

It is not, on the other hand, an easy city to find your way around in, as both Paris and New York are. Only the main avenues have names, and not many people bother to learn what they are, while house numbers are allotted on the basis not of location but of the time when they were built – their temporal rather than spatial relation to the other houses in the district. Yet if you hand a taxi driver an address in Japanese, chances are he will be able to find it; if he can't, he'll stop at the nearest police box and ask, for the police have a list, along with a map, showing the location of all the residents of their district. Of course, if you're going to one of the main hotels, or restaurants, or railway stations, or department stores, or some other well-known site, there's no problem – save a traffic jam or two.

Subway maps in English are readily available, and taking the subway often saves time, but if you're in Tokyo for only a short while, you probably won't want to go to the trouble of mastering the complications of the various lines and stations. Here again it must be noted that Japanese subways and trains have a clear and comprehensive system of signs in Roman letters as well as Japanese characters, so your chances of getting lost are not very great – unless you attempt to thread your way through some mammoth labyrinth like Shinjuku Station, where even natives of Tokyo often lose their way.

Central Tokyo is a bit like London in that it is made up of a number of wholly self-contained districts, with hotels, restaurants, bars, large department stores, and small shops, although many of the districts have special characteristics. Marunouchi, for example, is the financial center of the city and so is likely to be fairly quiet at night; Shinjuku, on the other hand, has more bars per square inch than any other part of the city and is never, never quiet at night.

SIGHTSEEING

Asakusa is another district that teems with bars, movie houses, and theatres, and it is also the site of Tokyo's favorite Buddhist shrine -- the temple dedicated to the Goddess of Mercy (Kannon). The area around the temple is famous for its souvenir shops. If you happen to be in Tokyo on one of the temple's festive days, brave the crowds and go up to see the great glittering palanquins being joggled through the narrow streets by hordes of chanting, panting young men. Despite destruction and reconstruction, Asakusa is probably nearer old Edo than any other part of Central Tokyo, though it is no longer the famous red-light district it once was.

A note to the unwary: Asakusa is not to be confused with Akasaka, a district with quite a different character. Although they seem so similar, the words are pronounced quite differently: the "u" in Asakusa is almost silent and the stress tends to fall on the second syllable, while every syllable in Akasaka has the same value and there is no noticeable stress.

Asakusa is a popular quarter, while Akasaka, along with its neighboring district of Roppongi, has some of the city's finest, as well as most expensive, restaurants and night clubs of all sorts. Many of the chief hotels are nearby, and it is quite a convenient neighborhood to stay in for a short visit.

So, of course, is the area around the Imperial Palace, which includes Marunouchi, where, if you are in Tokyo on business, you may well be spending much of your time. It is very near the Ginza, to a certain degree the modern heart of the city, and to Nihonbashi, the old center of Edo and still a very busy quarter, with three of Tokyo's large department stores within spitting distance of each other. The Ginza also has several department stores as well as innumerable specialty shops that cater to foreign visitors. Almost any shop in the Ginza will have at least one sales person who speaks English and probably some other foreign language as well.

Another quarter of great interest to the

tourist is Ueno, where many of Tokyo's chief
museums, including the famous National Museum, as well as the country's largest zoo are
located. The great private collections are scattered all over the center of the city, and one of
the best ways to decide which ones you want to
visit is to consult the list published every
Sunday in *The Japan Times*. It will tell you
what days and times they are open, most of
them are closed on Monday, as well as what
special exhibits are on display. One collection
you ought not to miss, even if the exhibit
happens not to interest you, is the Suntory
Museum, which occupies the ninth floor of the
Palace Building (next door to the Palace Hotel)
and offers a spectacular view of the gardens
and buildings within the Imperial Palace moat.

Another major sight is the shrine dedicated
to Emperor Meiji, with its beautiful gardens
and the nearby Meiji Park, which now houses
several of the installations put up for the
Olympic Games of 1964. These include the
National Stadium (which seats some 85,000),

two baseball stadiums, a football field, and a large indoor swimming pool.

But Tokyo is not only a huge city, with numerous sights of interest, it is also, as we have pointed out, a very confusing one, so we repeat our advice to have a look at the various tours available and choose the ones that are of interest to you. After all, if you feel you would have liked to spend more time at one or another of the places you visited, you can always return the following day. The porter at your hotel will translate your instructions for the taxi driver.

Both Nikko and Kamakura are places you can get to easily by yourself from Tokyo by train, but once you are there, you may find yourself overwhelmed by the confusing wealth of places of interest, so probably here again you would be well-advised to go with a group and a guide. Nikko is most famous for the opulent shrine dedicated to Tokugawa Ieyasu (built in the seventeenth century), while Kamakura's most famous site is the Great Buddha, cast in bronze in the thirteenth century, but both cities have a profusion of shrines, temples, gardens, and ornamental gates (*torii*) – and distances, as always, are formidable. Incidentally, if you plan to go to the beach at Kamakura or to the neighboring seaside on a midsummer weekend, be prepared for Coney Island on the Fourth of July -- and then some. One other word of caution: Nikko is in the mountains, and so the temperature there is always noticeably cooler than that of Tokyo. Further, if you go on a tour, you will be taken even further up, to Lake Chuzenji, which has magnificent scenery but a temperature that is likely to be downright cold, even on a hot day in Tokyo, so take a heavy sweater or coat.

Japan's other "must" – in fact, its chief "must" -- is of course Kyoto, the ancient capital. Getting there is easy. There are any number of daily domestic flights to Osaka (45 minutes), from which an express train will get you to Kyoto in thirty minutes. Or you can take JNR's New Tokaido Line (called the bullet train), which does the run between Tokyo and Kyoto in less than three hours. So, counting the time it takes to get to and from the airports, it's six of one and half a dozen of the other.

But the train has one advantage. You can get off at Nagoya (two hours from Tokyo by the super express) and from there make the much recommended pilgrimage to Japan's chief shrine, that at Ise, which is dedicated to the country's patroness, Amaterasu-Omikami, Goddess of the Sun and grandmother of the grandfather of the first emperor. The train from Nagoya to Ise takes an hour and eighteen minutes -- so you will almost certainly want to spend at least one night in Nagoya, where, as always in Japan, it is advisable to make your hotel reservation as far ahead as possible. In fact, it is advisable to plan your whole tour ahead, fix your dates, *and then stick to them.*

Nagoya itself, a city of nearly two million, it's Japan's third largest city, is not in itself of great interest, although there are certainly sights to see, many of them connected with the Tokugawa family, one branch of which lived in Nagoya until the Meiji Restoration of 1868. There is a castle built in 1612, there is the Tokugawa Art Museum, and there are a number of temples and shrines, including the Atsuta Shrine, founded in the third century and second only to Ise in importance because of its connection with the Sacred Sword, which, together with the Mirror at Ise and the Jewels at the Imperial Palace, constitute the Three Regalia of the Emperor.

At Ise, the Geku (or Outer Shrine) is considered to be almost as sacred as the Naiku (the Inner Shrine), and both are intimately associated with the ancient Shinto and the Imperial cult. Both also, incidentally, cover wide areas and consist of a number of buildings, along with gardens, ponds, and streams. The shrines are considered so sacred that visitors are not allowed beyond the first fence and are expected to remove their overcoats and hats when they stand in front of the shrines. On important holidays, such as New Year's, hundreds of thousands of Japanese make pilgrimages to Ise, so should your visit happen to coincide with some festive day, you must be prepared for crowds out of the ordinary. There is really never a time when the Ise shrines are deserted and the visitor can wander romantically about without bumping into another sightseer -- or a batch of them.

But probably it is no secret to anybody any more that the world is experiencing a population explosion, and that more and more of that exploding population is taking to the air, particularly now that the era of the jumbo jets has arrived. Japan, small and overcrowded, is no exception – but the tourist, as we have already pointed out, will probably be less annoyed by crowds here than in many other countries, for the Japanese have long ago learned to occupy the minimum of space themselves and at the same time to refrain from infringing on the spatial rights of others.

Osaka, with a population of over three million, is a bustling commercial center whose inhabitants have the reputation of being the shrewdest businessmen in the country.

The two great sites of ancient Japan are Kyoto and Nara. Nara was the first so-called "permanent capital" of the Japanese emperors. In the first few centuries after the founding of the Yamato court. it was customary for the emperors to choose a new capital on their accession to the throne – or when they felt that their old capital had, for one reason or another, become inauspicious. Then Buddhism took an ever firmer grip on the court, and as it did, the court became increasingly intrigued and influenced by mainland art and customs. Once Japan determined to imitate the elaborate court ritual of China, capital-hopping became unwieldy, and in the year 710 the Empress-Regnant Gemmyo made Nara her capital and such it continued during seven reigns until Emperor Kammu determined on a change.

Some say the Buddhist monks of Nara had grown so rich and powerful as to threaten the very existence of the throne; others, that Kammu had had his brother slain and felt that Nara was haunted by the uneasy spirit of the murdered prince. For whatever reason, Kammu determined first on a site a few miles southwest of Kyoto and then on Kyoto itself. He could hardly have chosen a better site: it was watered by two rivers and surrounded by mountains – "a natural sanctuary," the Emperor himself is said to have called it, and so an ideal place from which to rule a country that was by no means wholly pacified.

Having first secured the permission of the local Shinto deity, the emperor erected a temple northeast of where he intended to build his capital. As everyone knows, the northeast is the source of danger – and what better way to counteract the danger than to put a temple there? Once that was done, priests arranged that the new capital had the protection of the spirits of the four cardinal points. And finally, to the east, a colossal clay statue of a warrior was set up: it was his job, if enemy armies threatened the city, to give warning by singing as he moved toward the new capital.

Now Kammu was ready to begin building a city to house his palace. He laid it out according to the most advanced Chinese principles of town planning then available, and even today Kyoto presents an orderly appearance that helter-skelter Tokyo lacks. The city has, of course, grown enormously in its twelve centuries of life, over ten of them under imperial rule, but it still gives a unique picture of old Japan. Kammu's original capital was a rectangle, some six thousand yards on one side by five thousand on the other, all surrounded by an earthwork wall covered with tiles (called the *rasho*). There were many splendid gates ((*mon*), and if you put the two words together, you get the title of Japan's most famous motion picture.

The original name of the new city was Heian-kyò, the Capital of Peace, later it was changed to Kyoto, which comes from two Chinese characters that mean nothing more than The Capital. It has been estimated that even as long ago as the ninth and tenth centuries, there were only two European cities as large as Kyoto – Constantinople and Cordova. Today, of course, there are many larger cities, for Kyoto's population is less than a million and a half, yet few are so rich in historic association. Kyoto saw the birth and development of almost all the arts of Japan. Here too stands the imposing Imperial Palace, rebuilt time and again in the antique style, as well as one of Japan's most famous and admired structures, the Katsura Imperial Villa. Today the city has about fifteen hundred Buddhist temples and more than two hundred Shinto shrines. As might be expected, it has more religious festivals and processions than any other city of Japan.

For us to attempt to list and describe only the chief sights of a city like Kyoto would be beyond the scope of our little book. We have already mentioned the Imperial Palace and Katsura, neither of which you will want to miss – but these constitute, after all, only the barest beginning. Nowhere else in Japan will you see so many ancient temples and shrines, or temples and shrines rebuilt in the antique manner, many of them graced with paintings and sculptures that have been duly designated by the government as "national treasures" or "important cultural properties" and the like.

Yet these too are but a fraction of the sights to be seen in Kyoto — for the city, over many long centuries, has been the capital of much applied art, such as silk-weaving and dyeing, embroidery, manufacture of fine porcelain and lacquer, as well as doll-making. So once again we recommend, especially if you have but a few days to spend in Kyoto, that you make use of the excellent facilities of the Japan Tourist Bureau, which operates a number of morning, afternoon, and evening tours. You really cannot hope to see the major sites on your own unless you have virtually unlimited time — or unless, as we suggested earlier, you hire a car for the duration of your stay, along with a driver and a guide. The latter would, doubtless, be the best way to see Kyoto – but, as you have certainly learnt by now, the best things in life are not always free.

Nara, the more ancient capital, is well worth a visit, boasting almost as many important sights as Kyoto itself. The length of your visit must depend, of course, on the length of time you have at your disposal. You *can* do a one-day tour from either Kyoto or Osaka; or you could hole up and try to soak in the atmosphere of a not quite vanished Japan. Nara's most famous sight is, of course, the colossal bronze Buddha that was cast in the eighth century – and if you go home without seeing it, your friends may decide you were just playing around instead of attending to your proper business of sightseeing.

Just playing around, incidentally, is an awfully easy thing to do in Japan, for the Japanese play as industriously as they work. We shall make a few remarks on this subject a little later; let's keep the chapter on sightseeing clean.

SIGHTSEEING

Many Japanese will tell you that if you want to know the real Japan, you must get away from the cities, you must go into the countryside where there are no Western-style hotels, only Japanese inns (*ryokan*). There you will take your shoes off in the lobby, depositing them with the porter; you will be shown to a room with (chances are) straw matting on the floor, a low table with a few cushions around it, and perhaps nothing else; your maid will give you and your wife Japanese garments to wear during your stay – you don't *have* to wear them, but chances are you will, if only because you will soon decide they are more comfortable than the clothes you have on, and your wife will be delighted to wriggle out of her girdle. Your maid will serve you Japanese tea, which you may not like -- it won't taste a bit like Lipton's; and then you might decide to go down to the first floor and have a good soap and soak. You may find that men and women are sharing the same bath, or you may find that there are two baths with a wall between. The bath, incidentally, if you have chosen a hot springs, may well be the size of your swimming pool back home -- except that the water will be noticeably hotter. You will be an object of curiosity for a short while, perhaps only until you have proven that you know you're not supposed to leap into the bath until you've soaped and rinsed yourself; then, though you may be the only foreigners in sight, the Japanese will suspend their curiosity and return to the inner contemplation that a Japanese bath seems to invite.

Or you may be more adventurous still and go to a small village that is *not* a hot springs and that seldom sees foreigners from one year to the next. Here you will see what Japan was like once, before it began the process of transforming itself into one megalopolis -- and here also you will find that your **Instant Japanese** is invaluable, though it may not get you ham and eggs instead of bean paste or a soft down pillow instead of something that seems to have been cast by the nearest cement factory. Or if

153

it does get you ham and eggs, the ham may not taste like ham at all, it may taste more like what it really is – whale meat. But, despite the discomfort and occasional frustration, you won't forget that excursion into rural Japan – in fact, it may be with you vividly long after the temples of Kyoto, along with St. Peter's in Rome and Notre Dame de Paris, have faded away into an old-fashioned, sepia postcard.

As we noted above, Japan offers tremendous variety to the tourist who has time to spare: he can go to the north, to see the great snow festivals of Hokkaido, to ski during wintertime, to visit an Ainu village; or he can sail down Japan's lovely Inland Sea to Kyushu and continue on to its southeast tip, where the climate is more nearly subtropical; or he can make adventurous excursions into the more primitive world north of Tokyo that hovers around the Japan Alps. Wherever he goes, he will find unfailing courtesy, extraordinary kindness that he thought had vanished from the world long ago, and an interest that transcends the bounds of mere curiosity. He will, to be sure, occasionally meet unblinking stares, particularly among young girls, and hand-covered giggles – but, in compensation, he will also find that when he asks a direction, the person of whom he has asked it may drop whatever business he has in hand and personally conduct him to the desired place. He will have found, in a sense, a lost world, a world whose memory he will treasure as long as he lives.

6. FESTIVALS AND ANNUAL EVENTS

FESTIVALS AND ANNUAL EVENTS

You won't, of course, fix the dates for your Japan trip on the basis of some particular event, like a sumo tournament, but you might like to know a few of the highlights, so that if you're going to be in Japan at the time anyway, you can try to arrange your schedule to include any of the events that sound interesting to you.

First of all, you ought to know about Japan's national holidays, when just about everything is closed. These are:

New Year's Day (Janauary 1)
Adults' Day (January 15)
National Foundation Day (February 11)
Vernal Equinox Day (March 21 or 22)
Emperor's Birthday (April 29)
Constitution Day (May 3)
Children's Day (May 5)
Respect-for-the-Aged Day (September 15)
Autumnal Equinox Day (September 23 or 24)
Physical Education Day (October 10)
Culture Day (November 3)

Labor Thanksgiving Day (November 23)

Most of these holidays were established after the War to replace others that had a militaristic or excessively nationalistic flavor, for the occupying authorities, setting off their firecrackers on July Fourth, recognized that no country can get along without a certain number of holidays.

The period that begins with the Emperor's Birthday and ends with Children's Day is known as "Golden Week," because very often one or more of the three holidays touches a weekend, and then everyone gets a nice long vacation. (And don't dream of trying to go anywhere by train, unless you're willing to have somebody stand on your shoulders or vice versa; if you travel by car during Golden Week, be prepared to inch along.) Japanese firms don't, as a rule, give an annual two- or three-week vacation, as Western companies do, so Golden Week is often the employee's only chance for an extended hike, or some solid golfing, or skiing if the cold weather has held in the mountains, or swimming if the warm weather has come early — or just lying in bed and pretending there is no such thing as a subway during rush hours five or six times a week, and at the end of it a work-day that starts at nine and might end almost anytime. Being paid overtime is most unusual.

Another holiday for the Japanese -- and another date to note on your calender – occurs during the first week of January, when the whole life of the country shuts down. Offices and shops close; virtually the only restaurants that remain open are those in hotels that cater to foreigners; bars turn off their neon lights and padlock their doors, and waiters and waitresses and hostesses and mama-sans* take off their shoes and put their feet up. It is a

....

*"San" is a suffix that may be applied indiscriminately to men or women; it is the equivalent of Mr., Mrs., or Miss; when preceded by Mama, it usually means the proprietress of a bar.

boring time for the tourist, though, since there is literally nothing for him to do, and he would be well-advised to exclude the first week of January from his Japanese itinerary.

The Japanese, though few of them are Christians, have taken to Christmas in a big way, and the department stores have not been backward about exploiting this proclivity. During the month of December, if you go into one of the big department stores, there seem to be Christmas lights everywhere, and loudspeakers blare the familiar carols — though probably very few Japanese know or care what the words mean. We had quite a difficult time explaining to one employee that "I'm Dreaming of a White Christmas" had nothing to do with skin-color. The fact is, that the Japanese have found Christmas to be a pleasant diversion and have accepted it with their usual enthusiasm; they pay no more attention to the teachings that were later to be preached by the babe born in the manger than does the average Christian.

National holidays are but a small, and rather insignificant, part of the festival life of the country, which usually celebrates some shrine or temple deity or commemorates some important event in Japanese history. We append below a few of the more important events that are likely to be of interest to the foreigner; once again, space forbids an exhaustive list.

January 6 – *Dezome Shiki*. If you do happen to have spent that boring first week of January in Japan, here is your reward. You can go to the Outer Garden of the Meiji Shrine in Tokyo and see modern firemen re-enact those daring feats of agility on bamboo ladders that made the old fire-fighters of Edo so famous.

February 3 or 4 – *Setsubun*. This is the last day of winter, according to the lunar calendar, to celebrate which there are bean-throwing ceremonies all over the country – in shrines, temples, stores, etc. Some of the department stores make a big thing out of it, with costumed processions marching through the aisles. The best-known ceremony is at Shinshoji in Narita, Chiba Prefecture (about an hour and twenty minutes from Tokyo).

Also in early February is the famous snow festival in Hokkaido, when large, elaborately carved statues out of snow are set up along the main street of Sapporo.

May 12-15 – Grand Festival of the Myojin shrine in Kanda, Tokyo. The Kanda festival occurs only every other year, but if you happen to coincide with it, you would be well advised to brave the crowds, for it is a great favorite with the people of Tokyo, in order to see the enormous and elaborate palanquins being juggled through the narrow streets by scores of nearly naked boys. You would also be well-advised to take with you only the money you are likely to need for the morning or afternoon and to hold tight to your camera – for Tokyo, although its crime rate is considerably lower than that of most great Western cities, has its share of pickpockets and sneak thieves. Why tempt them?

May 15 – *Aoi Matsuri*. Literally "Hollyhock Festival," this is one of Kyoto's more interesting processions, A large number of people, dressed in ancient costume, proceeds from the Imperial Palace to the shrines, escorting an Imperial chariot decorated with hollyhocks and drawn by oxen.

May 18 -- Grand Festival of Toshogu Shrine at Nikko. Here, within easy distance of Tokyo, is another great procession in which some thousand people take part, all dressed in ancient costume. The procession is followed by contests in which "samurai" vie with each other in the old martial arts of Japan.

June 15 – Sanno Festival at Hie Shrine in Tokyo. This alternates with the Kanda Festival and vies with it in popularity. Both are much the same, with processions and palanquins, gilt, ornate, and very heavy, being jostled through the narrow streets by sweating, panting, shouting boys.

July 13-15 -- Bon Festival. Buddhist families light lanterns or fires in front of their houses to welcome their dead ancestors, who are thought to leave the next world and revisit this one during these days. There is also dancing, for the festival is joyful rather than sad.

July 17-24 – Gion Festival of Yasaka Shrine, Kyoto. Not only the most celebrated festival of Kyoto but of all Japan, this dates all the way back to the ninth century. On the first and last days of the festival, splendidly decorated floats parade through the main streets of the city, accompanied by the sound of flutes, drums, gongs, and the like. The floats are of two kinds: the *hoko*, a high tower on four enormous wooden wheels, and the *yama*, which contains a single figure or group of figures. Both require a large number of strong, high-spirited men to pull them. *Saké* is said to be of great help in this endeavor; beer, less so. On the festival of the 17th, there are reserved seats for visitors, and as the crowds are enormous, the visitor is advised to reserve his seat as far in advance as possible – and use it.

September 16 – *Yabusame*. This festival, which

takes place annually at the Hachiman Shrine in Kamakura, is rather small but is quite picturesque nonetheless. A group of around twenty horsemen, dressed in old-fashioned samurai hunting costumes, shoot arrows at a target from speeding horses. The festival is said to date from the twelfth century, when it was inaugurated in honor of the *kami* of the Hachiman Shrine.

October 22 – *Jidai Matsuri*. Another of Kyoto's many festivals, this is held to commemorate the founding of the city in 794; here there is a long procession of people dressed in costumes of the various periods of the city's ten centuries of Imperial occupation.

December 31 – *Omisoka*. During the course of the night, millions of people throughout Japan pay their respects to their ancestors at the major shrines in Tokyo and Osaka as well as at the Ise Grand Shrines. The Western tourist will probably be surprised to observe the difference between Christmas and New Year's Eve in his own country and the way they are observed in

Japan. The Westerner tends to think of Christmas as a family holiday and prefers to spend Christmas Eve at home; the Japanese, on the other hand, like to go barring or pub-crawling on Christmas Eve and nurse their hangover through Christmas Day. New Year's Eve, by contrast, is a family holiday in Japan, and Japanese young men and women who have left home to work in the large cities will travel enormous distances in order to spend that time with their parents.

We have listed relatively few of Japan's many, many festivals, choosing in particular those that are in, or within easy access of, Tokyo and Kyoto, where the tourist will spend most of his time. Any visitor who is particularly interested in this aspect of Japanese life need but make a call at the National Tourist Information Center, near the Ginza, where he will get all the information he desires. The daily English-language newspapers usually announce festivals too, but they are undependable: all too often they tell you about them after they are over.

7. SHOPPING

SHOPPING

What are we to tell you about shopping? You probably already have a list of things you want to buy -- and you probably already have an idea of how much you're prepared to pay for them. Insofar as the latter item is concerned, you're very likely in for a shock -- some of the things you wanted will seem to you outrageously expensive. Our only reply is that they are indeed expensive but that native Japanese pay the price, so why shouldn't you? The things that will strike you as virtually beyond the pale are embroidered silk kimonos, antique (or even modern) hand-decorated vases and bowls, and old chests of drawers (*tansu*) made with loving care by skilled craftsmen long before Japan decided to industrialize herself.

One other item the price of which will seem disproportionate is scrolls, decorated with painting or calligraphy. Here our advice is simplicity itself: unless you are a true connoisseur and know the field of Oriental art as well as, or better than, the dealer himself, pay only what you would be prepared to pay if the scroll were a modern copy. Japan has, literally, millions of such scrolls for sale, and only a man who has made Oriental art his life-work is in a position to distinguish the antique from the modern, the true from the false, the good from the bad. So if you see a scroll you like, and if the price seems right, buy it. Chances are it will be a modern copy, but if you didn't go bankrupt in the purchase, you won't mind, and once you get it home nobody will know the difference anyway.

The same strictures apply to *ukiyo-e* prints, which were produced in such prodigious quantities during the Edo Period that they were used as wrapping paper when Japan started trading with the West. Nowadays, they're far scarcer, and many of the ones you see in bookshops and print-shops will be modern copies of Hokusai and Hiroshige, but if you like the print and pay what you feel to be a fair price, what's the difference?

As for those sometimes wildly expensive, heavy silk, embroidered kimonos, you have a choice: there are specialty shops (many of them in the Ginza), and every department store has a floor devoted to kimonos – often, for some reason, the third. There is one difference: trying to bargain in a department store would be about as sacrilegious as playing your transistor radio in church. Small shops are more willing to compromise.

Much the same is true of those lovely chests of drawers (*tansu*) that blend so well with modern decor (and that are not really all that difficult to ship home -- the shop will, in fact, see to it for you). Many department stores have an antique corner, where you can buy not only *tansu* but old porcelain, silver teapots, and the like; and at the same time there are shops scattered over the city that specialize in *tansu*. Once you have made your purchase – i.e., agreed on your price -- you will find that the shops are utterly reliable: they will pack the chest carefully and see about insuring and shipping it. Should it fail to arrive, your insurance will protect you.

The department store (or *depâto*, as the Japanese call it) is in many ways a uniquely Japanese institution. They all have numerous exhibitions of paintings, pottery, tea utensils, dolls, and the like that usually last a couple of weeks and that are usually free ("a great waste of valuable space," as Macy's told Gimbel's); they all have a variety of eating-places, ranging from fairly expensive restaurants to snack bars; most of them have roof gardens where Mama can sit down and take her shoes off while the brats make use of slides and swings that are provided to divert them; the large department stores sell just about everything that's made in Japan and many imported articles – in fact, most department stores now have a high-fashion shop with a prestigious French name attached; they all (this will not interest you) have clubs where ladies can learn anything from doll-making to flower-arranging, and many organize excursions for club members and offer various sorts of easy-payment plans; most interesting of all to the Westerner is the fact that their prices are often higher than the little shop around the corner. Why then, since they are always crowded, do people patronize them? The fact is, many of the people crowding the narrow aisles aren't doing any patronizing at all – they're just having a family outing, and the hospitable, free, warm-in-winter, air-cooled-in-summer department store is as good a place as any. Anthropologists might find a parallel between the Japanese department store and Samuel Butler's musical bank in *Erewhon*.

The fact remains that if you want to see what Japan has to offer in the way of consumer goods, the department store is the place to begin. The larger ones are often eight-storied, with two or three basements and a roof garden. Almost invariably, one basement is devoted to foodstuffs, while another might be given over to household goods or bargain counters. All the larger stores have information desks just inside the various entrances, where young ladies will give you a floor plan of the store in English or, if your request is too difficult for them, will telephone up to the central information desk, where a fluent English-speaker will deal as best he or she can with your particular difficulty. When you finally do begin your hegira, smiling young ladies will bow you into either an escalator or an elevator. If, at that moment, you remember the malevolent ogresses who squirm behind information desks in American department stores and do their best to withhold any slight knowledge they may possess, you will smile back at the softly-murmuring young ladies. You won't bow -- although they will.

At the risk of favoritism, we feel obliged to point out that one department store – Takashimaya – makes shopping particularly easy for the non-Japanese-speaking foreigner. Takashimaya has a desk on the main floor where you may secure what is called a "Purchase Assembly Card." When you make a purchase, you don't hand out any money, you simply give the salesperson your card, and he or she will make a notation on it and take one of the little labels attached. Eventually, having been beguiled into buying far more than you intended, you return to the main floor desk and collect and pay for your purchases. Residents who have yen-acounts in local banks may give a personal check; tourists may use credit cards. Pity more department stores haven't realized that foreigners *do* get confused by strange Japanese ways and made it as easy for them to part with their money as Takashimaya does.

The largest department store in Tokyo is said to be the main branch of Mitsukoshi, at Nihonbashi, and perhaps it does indeed occupy more floor space than the others, but it is doubtful if the tourist will see any great difference between it and the other large stores in the Ginza or those at Shinjuku. They all have an overseas shipping department, which will save you coping with the capricious Japanese post office.

We have said nothing so far about the large and small specialty shops, and probably there is nothing to say save that those which cater to foreigners tend to cluster around the Ginza or in the Akasaka-Roppongi area. Cameras, radios, watches, silks, pearls, ceramics, bamboo ware, lacquer -- there are shops that specialize in all of them. And don't forget you'll want your passport with you to prove you're a dyed-in-the-wool tourist, so you can avoid the luxury tax that the rest of us have to pay.

You'll want to bear in mind, if you're buying FM radios and television sets, that channels differ. A Japanese televison set won't work in the United States unless it's one made especially for American channels. Similarly, FM frequencies in Japan are different from those in the United States, so you must always be sure that what you buy is a model designed for use in your own country. A tip to the adventurous: Japan doesn't go in much for those so-called "discount houses" so familiar to Americans, but there is one exception. If you get into a cab and say "Akihabara," you'll be driven to the district that specializes in all sorts of elec-

trical equipment and that sells it, incidentally, some thirty per cent less than the department stores do. What's more, you needn't accept the first price as the final one. The largest shop at Akihabara is Yamagiwa (it's a good place to begin), but there are hundreds of others, so if you have time and stamina enough, you can compare prices until you get the best bargain going. But, to repeat, don't get so excited by the bargaining that you buy a television or FM set intended for Japanese use -- it simply won't work when you get it home.

Japanese standard voltage, by the way, is 100 A.C., which is, for all intents and purposes, interchangeable with standard 110.

So far, we have given all our attention to shopping in Tokyo, but you may find some of the other cities you visit more rewarding. Kamakura, for instance, small as it is, probably has more antique shops than Tokyo itself: they tend to cluster in two streets, that leading to the Great Buddha and that which will eventual-ly get you to the Hachiman Shrine. Nikko too has a number of antique and souvenir shops and is famous for its carved wooden ware. We have already noted that Kyoto was the birthplace of most traditional Japanese art, and it is still a good place to shop for it. Try especially Shijo-dori, Shinkyo-goku (also called Kyo-goku), and the neighborhood around the main train station. In Nara, it's the main street, called Sanjo-dori.

Happy hunting!

And remember that Japan isn't all that different from the rest of the world. It's still "Caveat Emptor."

8. HAVE FUN

People amuse themselves in Tokyo in just about the same ways that they do all over the world. There are of course, a few exceptions that are peculiarly Japanese, but on the whole Tokyoites and their visitors eat and drink (and a lot of them get drunk), they dance and watch floor shows, and eventually, if they are lucky, they end up with the partner of their choice. The luck here is, of course, many-sided, and one aspect of it is that the legal and lawful spouse is not present. She may be back at the hotel nursing a bout of the flu, or maybe she was left behind in Peoria (how do you know what she's doing?), or she may simply be non-existent. In any case, whatever her status, she has not succeeded in interfering with the friendly relations between you and the girl who was suddenly sitting next to you at the bar and for whom you've been buying drinks (tea masquerading as whisky?) all evening. You are in luck, and probably your hotel, even if you happen to have a single room, won't say a word. If by any chance you have a double room and your wife is in it, nursing that bout of the flu, then the young lady will know any number of charming and expensive places to go.

We have, to be sure, begun this chapter with the lowest depths of depravity, and we have done it with a purpose. We are not suggesting that Japanese girls are pushovers; rather, they are friendly and easy-going (you must use a certain amount of judgment here), and they don't regard an evening's fun with a likable stranger as second only to matricide. Incidentally, if you happen to be a likable stranger in his fifties or sixties -- or even seventies, for pity's sake – you will find that young Japanese regard their elders with respect, not contempt, and they don't find a slap and tickle with an older man in any way demeaning. This will probably come as a pleasant surprise, indeed a delightful revelation, to middle-aged Americans whose children have already relegated them contemptuously to the dust-heap. If, on the other hand, you are a member in good standing of the Gideon Society and find such suggestions as we have just made not only offensive but disgusting, we would like to remind you that the Ueno Zoo is the largest in Tokyo, full of interesting specimens, and suitable for the entire family. Bear in mind also that it closes at dusk.

Nonetheless, you can still have fun in Tokyo without frequenting such haunts of sin as cabarets and night-clubs. There are theatres of all sorts and movie houses galore (with the first-runs showing the film in the original language); there is a tremendous variety of restaurants, ranging all the way from the food of some obscure Chinese district to a branch of Maxim's; and don't forget that after a long day of sightseeing, you might have the most fun putting your feet up and turning on the television set in your hotel room. Tokyo boasts seven channels, so you will probably be able to find something amusing; and if you can't, the spot advertisements will at least seem familiar.

But if you're going to do as Tokyoites do, then you'll have a full and replete night life.

HAVE FUN

One night you'll go to see the Flamenco dancers, another you'll have dinner at an Indian restaurant and then see a late show at one of the hotel night clubs. Another night you might just do a pub-crawl in the Ginza or Shinjuku areas, both of which boast so many drinking places you could probably spend a lifetime in either place without getting around to all of them. Further, you will find that pub-crawling is not an expensive pastime in Japan. Most ordinary bars charge around the equivalent of $1.50 for the national drink, which is whiskey (Japanese, of course) and water and which is called a *mizuwari*. Of course, if you insist on drinking imported Scotch or bourbon, you'll find you've spent quite a bit before the night is out. One kind of bar you ought very definitely to have a go at on your pub-crawl is one of the several huge drinking establishments run by the Suntory Company, makers of the country's most popular whiskey. A couple of the Suntory bars in the Ginza are so enormous that they house around a dozen ordinary-sized bars -- and if you should happen to wander in at a busy time (say, around eight in the evening) you might have trouble finding a seat at any of them. Your hotel porter will tell you how to find them or will give directions to a cab driver.

Be warned, however, that if you do your drinking in a hostess bar, your own drinks will be vastly more expensive and so will those of the charming young lady determinedly giggling at your jokes whether she understands them or not. In many such bars, you are expected to pay for the hostess's time; you may decide, looking at the size of the bill, that she should have been a company executive. One further word of warning: don't make a fuss about the bill in bars of this sort. They all employ sturdy young men whose business it is to see that you end up by paying what you owe; you'll have gained nothing but a loss of face.

Another form of entertainment that can run into money is doing the night club and cabaret circuit, many of them with entertainment *and*

hostesses, and sometimes the entertainment is topless but not the hostesses. Here again maybe your best bet would be to take a night tour. That way you can see what the city has to offer and go back to the type of place that you found most entertaining.

Two music halls popular with visitors are the Kokusai (in Asakusa) and the Nichigeki (in the Ginza, fourth floor of the Nichigeki Theatre Building). Both offer spectacles featuring the female youth and beauty of Japan, but where the Nichigeki goes in mostly for toplessness, the Kokusai is for the family. Aside from long rows of girls dancing in precision, it always offers at least one manifestation of nature that you would have thought unpresentable on any stage, such as a giant waterfall, an earthquake, or a three-alarm fire.

We've already noted that most districts of Tokyo have their own distinctive character, and one good way to discover what that character is to wander about the district at night going into bars and restaurants that catch your fancy. Give each district at least one night of its own -- if you have the time. And remember that the Japanese have their own way of doing things -- they're as likely to tuck a rathskellar up on a roof as to put an outdoor French café in a second basement! So if you want to sample the varied delights that Tokyo has to offer, don't stick to the ground floor. Be bold: wander up and down. It's most unlikely that you'll get into any trouble; Tokyo is probably the "safest" large city in the world. The worst that's likely to happen is that you'll find yourself paying an unexpectedly large bill, and after your anger wears off, you can chalk it down to experience.

Don't get the idea that the people of Tokyo do nothing with their evenings but eat, drink, and make passes at girls who wear contact lenses. A lot of them go to night school, where they work very hard trying to learn English, efforts that meet with all too little success, for their own language is simply too different from the languages of Europe. We're not suggesting a night school for you as a place to have fun of an evening, nor will you feel much at home in a mah jong parlor (even though your wife may have been a whiz back in the 'twenties') — but there are other diversions that don't require any alcoholic intake. Innumerable bowling alleys are scattered over the city, and they stay open until quite late, as do golf ranges, where you can practice driving.

In fact, you can probably find any sort of amusement in Japan's large cities that you could find in your own city back home (if it's large enough) — plus a few odds and ends that the Japanese have worked out for themselves. Take, for instance, their Turkish and Sauna baths (advertised in the English-language newspapers) where all the masseurs are masseuses, and young and pretty to boot. This is one excursion where you would be best advised to leave your wife at some nearby movie house; unfortunately for her, the Japanese haven't yet got around to providing Turkish baths for women with young and handsome masseurs.

But they will.

One exclusively Japanese form of "entertainment" that you had better leave alone is the geisha party -- unless you are forced to go to one by some Japanese acquaintance. After about fifteen minutes of it, of trying to get a mouthful of *saké* out of a cup that doesn't really hold a mouthful, of listening to jokes and chatter that you don't understand and would be bored by if you did, you'll want to leave. But that would be most improper. Geisha parties are among the most expensive forms of so-called entertainment in the world, one reason being that a geisha is not considered a true mistress of all her arts until she is about fifty, by which age she may command extremely high prices for pouring out *saké* with the utmost grace, never letting the conversation lag, being quick to pick up a pun and make another, and dancing and singing on occasion. The longer the party goes on, the more expensive it is, the more face your Japanese host acquires, and the more honor is being done to

you, so try to be philosophical about it – it's
bound to end sometime.

And so, by the way, is this book.

9. A FEW USEFUL PHRASES

A FEW USEFUL PHRASES

In this section, we don't intend that you attain instant fluency in the Japanese language. Learning, or at least, using these few phrases might ease you over a rough spot or two, and will show your friends in Japan that you made an effort.

Despite the fact that the Japanese make a great point of their ineptness at English, you will be surprised at how many know a number of essential words in the language. If you follow the rule of sweet-simple-slow, you can get a recognition signal in many basic situations. Stick to nouns as much as possible, avoid puns and slang like the plague, and confine your humor to the back-slapping, banana-peel variety.

Japanese is polysyllabic, each syllable either a vowel or a single consonant-vowel combination. L and R are the same sound to the Japanese ear and tongue, and there is no V or TH sound. You'll have to recognize the attempts to approximate these sounds.

See the companion volume to this book.

A FEW USEFUL PHRASES

INSTANT JAPANESE, for more thorough guidance in the use of the Japanese language. But forge ahead and try the following on your friends.

Mr., Mrs., Miss	-san (Smith-san, Tanaka-san)
Hello. Good day	Konnichi wa
Good morning	O-hayo
Good evening	Komban wa
Goodbye	Sayonara
How are you?	Ogenki desu ka
Yes	So desu
No	Iie (rather abrupt, seldom used)
Excuse me	Gomen nasai
Where is ———?	——— doko desu ka?
How far? How long?	Dono kurai?
How much? (price)	Ikura desu ka?
Why?	Naze desu ka?
When?	Itsu desu ka?
Which?	Dochira desu ka?

A FEW USEFUL PHRASES

What?   Nani de suka?
   (you will now have noticed that *ka* is the
   question mark spoken, desu is the verb for
   to be, am, is)

One   Hitotsu
Two   Futatsu
Three   Mittsu
Four   Yottsu
Five   Itsutsu
Six   Muttsu
Seven   Nanatsu
Eight   Yattsu
Nine   Kokonotsu
Ten   To
Eleven   Ju-ichi
Twelve   Ju-ni
Twenty   Ni-ju
Thirty   San-ju
Forty   Yon-ju
Fifty   Go-ju
Sixty   Roku-ju
Seventy   Nana-ju

A FEW USEFUL PHRASES

Eighty	Hachi-ju
Ninety	Kyu-ju
One hundred	Hyaku
One thousand	Sen
Ten thousand	Man
Million	Hyaku-man
Taxi	Takushi
Train	Densha
(Bullet train	Shinkansen)
Automobile	Jidosha
Airplane	Hikoki
Subway	Chikatetsu
Take me to ——	—— e annaishite kudasai
What time is it?	Nanji desu ka?
Noon	Shogo
One p.m.	Gogo Ichiji
Two p.m.	Gogo Niji
Three p.m.	Gogo Sanji
Four p.m.	Gogo Yoji
Five p.m.	Gogo Goji
Six p.m.	Gogo Rokuji

A FEW USEFUL PHRASES

Seven p.m.	Gogo Shichiji
Eight p.m.	Gogo Hachiji
Nine p.m.	Gogo Kuji
Ten. p.m.	Gogo Juji
Eleven p.m.	Gogo Juichiji
Midnight	Yoru no Juniji
One a.m.	Gozen Ichiji
Two a.m.	Gozen Niji
Three a.m.	Gozen Sanji
Four a.m.	Gozen Yoji
Five a.m.	Gozen Goji
Six a.m.	Gozen Rokuji
Seven a.m.	Gozen Shichiji
Eight a.m.	Gozen Hachiji
Nine a.m.	Gozen Kuji
Ten a.m.	Gozen Juji
Eleven a.m.	Gozen Juichiji
Six fifteen	Rokuji jugo fun sugi
Six thirty	Rokuji han
Six forty-five	Shichiji jugo fun mae
Today	Kyo
Yesterday	Kino
Day before yesterday	Ototoi

A FEW USEFUL PHRASES

Tomorrow	Ashita
Day after tomorrow	Asatte
This week	Konshu
Next week	Raishu
Cigarettes	Tabako
Whisky	Uisuki
Beer	Biiru
Tea (green)	Ocha
(black)	Kocha
Coffee	Kohi
Breakfast	Asa Gohan
Lunch	Hiru Gohan
Dinner	Ban Gohan
Please (for benefit of speaker)	Kudasai (after verb)
Please (for benefit of person spoken to)	Dozo
Thank you.	Domo Arigato (usually Domo is sufficient)
Don't mention it.	Do ita shimashite
My wife	Kanai
Your wife	Okusan

A FEW USEFUL PHRASES

Son	Musuko
Daughter	Musume
Book	Hon
Magazine	Zasshi
Bookshop	Hon-ya
Newspaper	Shimbun
English language	Eigo
Japanese language	Nihongo
Monday	Getsu Yobi
Tuesday	Ka Yobi
Wednesday	Sui Yobi
Thursday	Moku Yobi
Friday	Kin Yobi
Saturday	Do Yobi
Sunday	Nichi Yobi
January	Ichi Gatsu
February	Ni Gatsu
March	San Gatsu
April	Shi Gatsu
May	Go Gatsu
June	Roku Gatsu
July	Shichi Gatsu
August	Hachi Gatsu

A FEW USEFUL PHRASES

September	Ku Gatsu
October	Ju Gatsu
November	Juichi Gatsu
December	Juni Gatsu
New Years	O Sho Gatsu
Hotel	Hoteru
Room	Heya
Office	Jimusho
Company	Kaisha
America	Amerika (Beikoku)
American (Person)	Amerika Jin (Beikoku
Australia	Osutoraria Jin)
Australian (Person)	Osutoraria Jin
England	Eikoku
Englishman	Eikoku Jin
Japan	Nihon (Nippon)
Japanese	Nihon Jin (Nippon Jin)
Laundry	Sentaku
Fast	Hayai
Slow	Yukkuri
Barber	Tokoya
Beauty Shop	Biyoin
Doctor	Oisha

A FEW USEFUL PHRASES

Dentist	Haisha
Hot	Atsui
Cold	Samui